Magnificent, Rational, Strange

A beginner's guide to the universe

Magnificent, Rational, Strange

A beginner's guide to the universe

Ian Breckenridge

**IFF
BOOKS**

Winchester, UK
Washington, USA

JOHN HUNT PUBLISHING

First published by iff Books, 2021
iff Books is an imprint of John Hunt Publishing Ltd., No. 3 East Street, Alresford,
Hampshire SO24 9EE, UK
office@jhpbooks.com
www.johnhuntpublishing.com
www.iff-books.com

For distributor details and how to order please visit the 'Ordering' section on our website.

Text copyright: Ian Breckenridge 2020

ISBN: 978 1 78904 224 5
978 1 78904 225 2 (ebook)
Library of Congress Control Number: 2018954962

Design: Stuart Davies

UK: Printed and bound by CPI Group (UK) Ltd, Croydon, CR0 4YY
Printed in North America by CPI GPS partners

We operate a distinctive and ethical publishing philosophy in
all areas of our business, from our global network of authors to
production and worldwide distribution.

Contents

By the same author

Reclaiming Jesus: Making sense of the man without the miracles
published by O-Books in 2011

Have you ever wanted to understand the universe?
Once that desire burns away at your soul – really burns –
there's no going back.

Michael Brooks

Dear Reader

This book conveys something of the scale and sweep
of the universe we know today.
It examines not just the stars and galaxies
but the whole thing,
space and time, matter and light,
life and consciousness, reason and language.
It brings all this together in one volume, one picture
and invites us to give it some time and thought.

What sense might we make of it?
What might it make of us?

Do join me on this roller-coaster,
this voyage like no other.

Ian Breckenridge

Describing the indescribable

This book will sometimes struggle to find words which can do full justice to its extraordinary subject. Quite often it will be tempting to fall back on words like 'fantastic', 'colossal', or 'breathtaking', but superlatives like these, repeated too often, may eventually wear thin and lose much of their force. Some of the time, surrounded by wonders, it might even be better to understate things.

Similarly it will be tempting to attribute truly awe-inspiring phenomena to some supernatural force. This might appear to be a simple response, but it might also seem like giving up the quest altogether, and missing its strange magnificence. This book, however, will follow reason and evidence as far as they will take us.

This book, then, will try to limit itself to the reality of the material world, leaving other realities – moral, psychological, aesthetic, theological – as far as possible to one side.

Acknowledgements

This book is the end product of half a lifetime's obsession. During the past thirty years and more I have been learning with rising enthusiasm about the extraordinary place we find ourselves in. I hope that some of the excitement of this experience, this voyage, comes across to the reader.

I acknowledge the role of the many books which opened my understanding during these years. These are listed at the end of this book. For maybe twenty years I have also been an avid reader of the popular scientific press, notably the always accessible, always challenging *New Scientist* magazine.

My thanks to friends who have read the script, spotted errors and commented on factual and stylistic points – Pete Belton, Alan Berry, Toni Berry, George Breckenridge, Aubrey Hill,

David Knighton, Luzie Wingen.

Finally my love and gratitude to Beryl, who gave me the space to take this on and to see it through.

Embarking

A glance through the book

During the last several decades, within a little more than the span of a human life, we have created a new picture of this surrounding reality of ours in immense detail, from the Big Bang and black holes to the double helix and the genome, from the Large Hadron Collider and the geological history of planet earth to the private life of the brain and the deep history of our own species. The sciences, indeed, continue to open up new worlds at an exhilarating pace.

Excellent books have appeared on a whole array of particular topics. A smaller number cover a very much wider canvas, like the scale of cosmology, for example, or the evolution of life on earth, but surprisingly few titles have investigated the entire picture in one volume. By this I mean not just atoms, planets and galaxies, but the exquisite choreography of life, the intimate mystery of time, the puzzles of infinity and deep complexity, strange kinship of matter and energy, and the biochemical wizardry underwriting the human quest to make sense of all this.

This book ponders all of this. It sets out on a voyage into our 21st century universe, examining many of its wonders, but also probing its depths and asking what it might all add up to.

The first half of the book ranges from the world within each atom, through the stars and galaxies to the origin of all things. For some readers this may turn out to be stranger than they had expected. This universe is certainly rational but also unimaginably vast and impenetrably complex. Strangest of all, the whole thing emerged apparently from nowhere at a datable time in the past.

In its second half the book goes on to investigate the distinctive self-assembling system we know as life, with its baffling intricacy and its exceedingly ancient heritage. At some time several thousand million years ago early versions of life first took root and multiplied on a still young planet. Its complex molecular building blocks, moreover, may have been coming into place a good deal further back, before the sun ignited and the earth and the moon formed.

The book finally considers the consciousness by means of which we have been pondering all this, and the brain which generates, edits and supervises this whole experience. For some people this stands out as the most remarkable wonder of them all.

By the end of the book we will have come full circle – we start and we will finish with these inquisitive creatures looking up at the night sky, clumsy newcomers with their words and numbers, who so badly need to make sense of things.

Why might a book like this matter?

Within the last century, then, the picture we have of our universe has been transformed by spectacular advances in a whole range of sciences. A growing number of people are now beginning to see just how absolutely extraordinary this is. The emergence of this new understanding might in fact prove to be one of the truly great turning points in all of human history. It feels like an awakening.

Yet probably only a few of us, I imagine, will have taken the time to sit down and think this right through. This book gives you an opportunity to do that. So this book is not a coffee table 'gee-whizz' book, to be skimmed in one evening, nor indeed a pocket encyclopedia, but rather an invitation to reflect more carefully. For this truly is a voyage like no other, crossing a vast, wild territory, by turns both exhilarating and disorienting.

A unique adventure like this, then, might be uniquely rewarding. And in any case, if we are to call ourselves well-informed human beings in our own time, don't we need to be more aware of this reality which surrounds us? Don't we owe it to ourselves to try to make some sense out of it?

But there may be more to it than that. Our day-to-day working model of the universe by now probably lags behind this 21st century reality, perhaps by some distance. Perhaps more worryingly, our working model of ourselves may have become similarly out of date.

This surely matters to us rather urgently in our own time. In this century humanity is facing a whole series of challenges, from mass migration to climate change, from the poisoning of air, land and sea to the quiet rise of ever smarter robots. These challenges do question at a fundamental level exactly who we think we are, and today's headless exploitation of the earth, damaging the very biosphere on which we all depend, will surely no longer do as an answer. Maybe it's high time we took a fresh look at the whole picture, a long view, and considered what it might be telling us.

When we embark on a voyage like this, then, who knows what we might discover? We might even catch a glimpse, a clue to who we are and who we might become.

Maps of the territory

The first map looks up and out as we voyage into the world of our neighbouring stars and the galaxies beyond. Starting with the everyday marvel of our sun, we steer out through the solar system, past our nearest stars, out to the confines of our night sky. Beyond this we become aware of the surrounding apparition of the Milky Way. But we have barely started. And we soon realise the strangeness of this map as we begin to sense the eerie interweaving of time and space.

A second map looks in and down, through all the levels of physical reality, all the way down to the atom and the quantum world within it. This entire material universe, we realise, arises out of an exquisitely strange world deep within every atom.

Further maps look at the epic sweep of animal and plant life as it spread across the earth during the most recent half billion years or so. Its beauty and its diversity entrance us, from orchids to blue whales, from the leopard to the dragonfly. Yet the survival of life was never guaranteed, indeed it was mortally threatened by a series of catastrophes, the worst of them requiring some millions of years to effect a full recovery. Indeed the very survival of today's great panoply of life on earth, including our own species, is itself an unlikely wonder.

Yet it is easy to forget the earlier wonder of the evolution of the first living cells during the preceding three billion years. And even this wonder is perhaps in the end eclipsed by the emergence of the very earliest precursors of life, perhaps protected in the depths of the newly formed oceans at some point during the earth's first billion years.

A final map comes back to the creature who is drawing up the maps. All the workings of the human mind, from the most familiar daily routines to the deepest musings on the meaning of our existence, rest on neural systems of truly unimaginable complexity. Different biochemical catalysts take different fountain pathways through the geography of the brain, combining to influence our responses in a thousand ways every microsecond of our lives.

Natural voyagers

The remarkable thing is, the modern quest to understand this surrounding reality of ours once had ancient roots set deep within that reality itself. The first dim awakenings reach back at least a couple of million years to the heyday of our human predecessor Homo erectus. This is when the earliest precursors of modern human reason were presumably first shaped. Later, the voyage continued through what might be called the dream time of Homo sapiens, the 2–3 hundred millennia of early modern humanity when the first prototypes of language may have emerged. Later still it was further refracted through the very different, revolutionary times of Neolithic and early classical experience, with the emergence of agriculture, the first long-distance trading networks, the spread of writing and numbers, and the earliest truly destructive wars.

Much more recently this adventure entered a new phase as late renaissance science started to uncover more and more of the magnificent rationality of the universe. For an exhilarating period this seemed to be like a fully determined, rational machine which one day we would no doubt decode completely. In still more recent times, however, amid increasingly awesome discoveries there has emerged a very different picture, more like a great encompassing riddle than a machine.

In the last half-millennium, then, you could say this human voyage has taken us from an ancient infancy marked by all-pervading ignorance and fear, then through childhood wonder and growing adolescent confidence to today's more sober, thoughtful encounter. The question is, where will this voyage take us now?

Theme 1

The scale of reality

Chapter 1

Through the circle of the night

We now know that our universe is built on a truly stupendous scale, altogether vaster than anyone could have imagined just a handful of centuries ago. People today are becoming aware of this in a general sense but are still perhaps a bit vague on some of its major features. Perfectly intelligent individuals can even find themselves occasionally mixing up the solar system with our home galaxy, the Milky Way, and others sometimes confuse this one galaxy with the whole creation.

Looking back, the universe understood by Copernicus and Newton was still built on a broadly human scale. It was the 18th century astronomers, and then the founders of geology in the late 18th and early 19th centuries who probably first understood that this universe must be built on much more awesome dimensions. By the mid-19th century Darwin's extraordinary insight into the evolution of all living things dramatically confirmed this, but by the early decades of the 20th century even Darwin's dimensions had begun to look decidedly cramped. So when people today speak about the vastness of the universe, what do they mean exactly? How vast is vast?

A recent press article came up with an answer of a kind, estimating the number of atoms in the entire universe – 10 to the power 80, that is, one with eighty noughts after it (just for comparison, a billion has nine noughts after it). But a number like this is simply unimaginable. How can we possibly picture this scale of things?

In order to get our heads round this maybe we need to free up our imagination a little. Imagine then, if you will, a spacecraft advertising trips to the end of the universe (perhaps in the spirit of Douglas Adams' *Hitchhiker's Guide*). You have booked a seat, all the passengers have boarded, and we are ready for take-off. You recall that when you bought your ticket you were warned that this journey might be unsuitable for persons of a nervous disposition. But now the seat belts have been checked, you settle back, and off we go.

Our backyard

Our sun (sun swims into view) is such a familiar, daily presence that we might sometimes think of it as quite close, but in reality it is a long way off – some 149,600,000 kilometres distant from us in fact. Light travels at almost 300,000 kilometres per second, that is, seven and a half times round the earth in the time it takes you to read just a few words in this text, so the light which we see from the sun has taken 8 minutes and 20 seconds to reach us. That is, we see it as it was 8 minutes and 20 seconds ago. We express this by saying that the sun is 8 light minutes and 20 light seconds distant from us. (Our moon, just for comparison, is 1.28 light seconds distant from us.) Measured by our homely earthbound dimensions our planet is a very long way out from the sun – a modern spacecraft, travelling at well beyond the speed of sound, would take several months to reach the sun.

Light circumnavigates this earth, then, in 140 milliseconds, barely the time it takes to register an individual word as you read this sentence. This may be worth just a moment's pause for reflection. Light, part of the fabric of this universe, is a familiar element in our daily experience and yet it clearly operates on a scale far removed from us.

But on with our voyage. Our nearest neighbour Mars is approximately 227,940,000 kilometres, in other words between 12 and 13 'light minutes' distant from the sun. Hold on tight now, we're going up! Jupiter, the first of the so-called gas giants as we go out from the sun, is some 43 light minutes distant from the sun, while Saturn is between 79 and 80 light minutes away. Far away Pluto is 328 light minutes, in other words between

5 and 6 'light hours', or almost one-quarter of a 'light day' distant. NASA's craft 'New Horizons' took off from earth in 2006. Travelling at an average speed of 36,000 miles per hour, it took nine years to reach Pluto, arriving in July 2015.

We live in an age of discovering our solar system, recalling the age of discovering the earth in past centuries, and in recent years we have been getting used to its many splendours. We can for example admire the spectacular beauty of that designer masterpiece Saturn with its 62 moons and 7 bands of rings, as we view from space the flickering auroras around the mysterious rotating hexagonal cloud pattern in its north polar region. We can read about the thousand mile-deep vortex within its gas layer. We can admire the mile high water geysers on its tiny 300 mile-wide moon Enceladus.

At the centre of this planetary system burns the awesome furnace of the sun, a fierce, angry tumult of nuclear fire, spinning on its own axis, spitting arcs of flame far into surrounding space. The mind can register the facts of this but may perhaps find it hard to really grasp the fearful internal dynamics keeping this furnace in equilibrium. We are told that it is about midway through its ten billion year life cycle. By now, though, even junior school pupils know that our sun is just one star among countless others.

Our solar system, for all its power and splendour, is really no more than our immediate backyard, all its planets circling well within a light-day from the sun. What do we find when we venture out from this close compass? If we travel out well beyond the planet Uranus, the outermost of the four gas giants, and beyond even distant Pluto, we eventually reach the edge of the heliosphere, where the solar magnetic field finally peters out. This is between 17 and 18 light hours distance. Persevering out far beyond this we run in due course into the so-called Oort Cloud, not a cloud but an uncounted myriad of asteroid-like rocks somewhat chaotically circling our sun, anything from 50 light days all the way up to a bit more than a light year distant. People have calculated that the Oort Cloud probably has more mass than the rest of the solar system put together, including the sun.

Continuing still further out, our sun's nearest neighbour of significant size, Proxima Centauri, visible in southern latitudes, is 4.2 light years distant. The brightest star anywhere in the night sky, Sirius, outshining all the rest in the northern winter evening sky, is our second nearest neighbour, at a distance of 8.3 light years. There are in fact 11 sizable stars within 25 light years distance from us, and around 150 within the span of 100 light years. Many of the stars visible to the naked eye in our night sky are a few hundred light years distant from us, some as far as a few thousand light years away.

Many of us by now have got used to the remarkable fact that as we look out at the night sky we are looking back in time – the further out we look, the longer it has taken the light to reach us. This means that in our imagination we can link the stars we see in the night sky with our own history back on earth. So, where were you 4.2 years ago, when the light from our nearest star, Proxima Centauri, set out towards us? What was happening in world history 250 years ago, when the light set out from Bellatrix, one of the main stars in the constellation of Orion? At that time there were still 13 British colonies in North America. Going further out, the light from Deneb, in the Swan constellation high overhead in the northern summer evening sky, set out 2,600 years ago, before Socrates was born.

As far as the eye can see
But the stars we can see at night are in reality quite close neighbours. If the solar system is our backyard, then all the stars we can see in the night sky with the naked eye, taken together, could be compared perhaps to our local parish or maybe a suburban neighbourhood. In fact we can picture our night sky,

with its few hundred major stars, as like a small spherical patch of space with our sun and its midge-like attendant planets at its centre, the whole thing just a few thousand light years across, really quite an intimate little locality when you compare it to its immediate surroundings. Our solar system, then, sits at the centre of our night sky, and this night sky in turn is situated... somewhere within a very much grander affair.

Countless billions of more distant stars are visible to the naked eye as a faint continuous grey blur, arching high across our night sky, the Via Lactea (i.e. Milky Way) as our Roman forebears called it. What we are seeing is our own galaxy, an enormous flattened disc in shape a bit like a dinner plate, only we are seeing it from the inside. It encircles us, and the whole thing is turning on its own axis like a gigantic Ferris wheel. This wonder of the night sky is at its clearest before the moon has risen or after it has set, or perhaps at around the time of the new moon. The sky has to be really dark to see it at its best. As we gaze up at this silent encompassing apparition in the early evening sky it emerges from its background only slowly. But soon, if we keep watching, it appears eerily to draw closer to us as the eye becomes accustomed to the growing darkness. Instinctively we shiver as the hairs rise on the back of the neck.

How can we take our bearings within this giant spiral presence? As we look due south just above the horizon in the northern summer evening sky and recognise the pattern of stars sometimes called the teapot in the constellation of Sagittarius, we are looking towards the centre of our galaxy. Then if we locate the great spectacle of Orion with his belt, sword and bow dominating the southern sky on northern winter evenings, we are looking outwards, towards the edge of the galaxy. Our star, the sun, is located somewhere about halfway out from the centre of the galaxy on one of its several spiral arms roughly 25 thousand light years from the hub and a similar distance from the edge. Our galaxy is also about a thousand light years thick, which is why we see so many stars in areas of the sky far from the arc of the Milky Way itself. The whole galaxy may contain many score billion stars – estimates do vary.

Recently observers measuring the precise movements of the stars in the Milky Way relative to each other have concluded that the whole galaxy is rippling like a flag in the wind, just one stately ripple lasting a few million years. We are also told that the whole thing is revolving in a cycle completed every 210 million years. This means that the great extinction of the dinosaurs on earth some 65 million years ago happened, we could say, almost a third of a galactic cycle ago. Likewise the evolution of multi-celled life on our planet, life as we know it, got underway just some 600 million years ago, in other words almost three galactic revolutions ago. The formation of our local solar system out of spiralling rock, ice and dust happened in an unremarkable corner of the galaxy approximately 4.5 billion years ago, that is, just over 21 galactic revolutions ago. Finally the whole galaxy itself, at some ten billion years in existence, will soon be on the countdown to complete 47 revolutions. Only 47 – at last among all these zillions we have a number we can relate to.

Light, meanwhile, shoots across our galaxy in a mere 100 thousand years. So if we are 25 thousand light years from its centre, then I suppose light from its far side will have taken something like 75 thousand years to reach us. This light, then, must have started out when early Homo sapiens, our human ancestors, lived in Africa, perhaps only a few millennia before some of them first crossed to Asia at the very start of their migration across the continents.

One way or another, here we are, perched out on one of our galaxy's spiral arms, in the middle of, well, heaven only knows where.

Deep space

Yet our voyage has still some way to go. Everything we can see as we gaze up at the night sky is part of the Milky Way, our own galaxy – everything, that is, except three objects. In the skies of the southern hemisphere two faint grey smudges can be picked out, known historically as the Smaller and Larger Magellanic Clouds. (Did the 16th century voyager Magellan record these strange apparitions as he attempted the first global circumnavigation, sailing into the southern oceans and then westwards across the Pacific?) We now recognise these 'clouds' as two relatively small galaxies which are in effect satellites of our own Milky Way, situated 160,000 and 200,000 light years away respectively, yet still drawn by the immense gravitational pull of their larger neighbour as it turns on its axis. These two Magellanic galaxies are in fact the largest of some twenty so-called dwarf galaxies broadly within the gravitational field of the Milky Way.

Then in our northern skies, still rising in the east in an autumn evening, is another faint smudge, located not far above and to the left of the great rectangle of Pegasus. We now know this as the Andromeda Galaxy, our closest neighbouring galaxy, about 2.4 million light years distant from us and now reckoned to be quite a bit larger than the entire Milky Way. That would make it the largest object visible to the naked eye, larger in fact than everything else we can see put together.

By now, though, we have reached the limits of what the human eye can see unaided. Now it's time to engage one final gear-shift as we turn to our on-board telescopes and find ourselves emerging clear from the Milky Way itself. Quite soon it becomes clear that both galaxies, our own and the Andromeda Galaxy, are members of a group of galaxies, some fifty or so including the attendant dwarf galaxies around some of them, whose distances from us are anything up to a few score million light years. Fully six of them can be seen by earth-based telescopes through the constellation of Virgo. One particularly gorgeous one, the so-called Whirlpool Galaxy, a favourite in astronomy calendars on sale before Christmas, is about 28 million light years distant. Taken together these galaxies are sometimes referred to as the 'home' group! Yet none of them, apart from Andromeda and the two Magellanic dwarf galaxies, is visible to the naked eye – they are simply too faint and too far away.

Yet this home group is well named. In the early decades of the twentieth century, as ever more powerful telescopes probed farther and farther into the deeper recesses of space, Edwin Hubble and his colleagues made a truly momentous discovery, transforming forever our view of the universe. More and more galaxies, hundreds then thousands of them, came into focus. The thousands soon became millions. Eventually it became clear that our universe consists of perhaps 100–200 billion galaxies, each with on average several hundreds of millions of stars. Many of these galaxies are relatively 'close' to us, others at distances stretching out to 12 billion light years and more. In recent years the broad patterns and networks of these galaxies have been partially mapped out. Astronomers describe these using words like clusters and superclusters, threads, mats, knots and voids.

The furthest detectable signals come from 13.8 billion light years distance. If we assume that our galaxy is approximately midway (more of this later), this would mean that the observable universe is some 27.6 billion light years across. This, then, does seem to be the scale on which this creation of ours is built.

Reflection: the logic of insignificance?

I suspect that our culture today still hasn't really digested this. Set within our own local galaxy our sun now looks lost, just one slightly above average star among such a scattering of numberless brilliance. Even our galaxy in all its grandeur seems equally lost in a sea of countless surrounding galaxies. What, then, does this make of us on our little blue planet, spinning along somewhere in deep space like a lost spacecraft? If even the solar system dwarfs us, and it assuredly does, the Milky Way does seem to obliterate any remaining importance we may have once thought we had. But when we contemplate this multibillion light year phenomenon, all our attempts to find meaningful comparison seem to go out of the window. Are we as insignificant as it is possible to get? Seen against this backdrop, yes it certainly looks like it.

Perhaps we are left feeling a bit dazed, not knowing exactly what to make of it all. No doubt we are astonished. Then perhaps we may feel a distinct chill, a discomfort, and on occasion we might even catch a whiff of an experience from early childhood, the rising panic of being utterly lost. Just a moment later, however, a quite different sense may come to us, an unmistakable sense of admiration. We are impressed, not to say awestruck at the undeniable magnificence of all this.

In the light of this, then, what on earth are we to make of ourselves? Are we just unimportant specks lost in the immensity of space, or are we something else as well, alongside that? There is, after all, something unmistakably epic about this. And when we come to think of it, this sense of our insignificance is in fact a reflection, is it not, of the grandeur of the whole thing. We can see both sides of this. If every last thing in this universe is equally insignificant and at the same time equally the inheritor of its spectacular magnificence, then this surely would apply to us too.

So maybe there is something remarkable about us after all, remarkable in the same way that everything in this universe is remarkable. To see this is to see that we are true expressions of this creation, unconsciously reflecting back its dazzling glory simply by being who we are.

But maybe we are also special in a way which may be unique to us. The astonishing fact is that we can actually capture this vast creation in our net of words, spelt out in code in this remarkable organ just above and behind the nose. And as we do this, and wonder at how we have managed to do it, we might, who knows, find one clue to the puzzle of who we are. As a species, after all, we really do need to make sense of things – understanding our world does matter to us, quite urgently in fact.

Interestingly, recent neurological research has suggested that this experience of awe and of our own insignificance can actually change us, making us less cynical and self-obsessed, and more ready to express sympathy and generosity towards others. It appears that the two brain circuits which activate the experience of awe and generosity may in fact be connected. Again, when we come to think of it, this is perhaps hardly surprising, given the maze of connections in the brain. (We'll come back to that later in the book.) It's as if our encounter with this universe can inspire us, can open us up to grander dimensions beyond ourselves.

One point may bear repetition. We can now see that space and time are strangely interwoven. This means that as we travel back through millions, then billions of years, galaxies come into view at earlier and earlier stages of formation, and eventually we see the very earliest stars just in the process of forming. Then, as we keep going on out beyond even this... nothing. We are looking at a time before the first galaxies formed, even before the very first stars ignited. Then if we keep going still farther out we get from our instruments something like a background noise, the so-called cosmic microwave background. It is as if we have come up against an outer wall, from which a faint echo comes back to us. Could this be the echo of the birth moment of everything, of all that is?

Our voyage has apparently arrived, not at the end of the universe, but rather at its beginning. All the while our map has been not three- but four-dimensional. At this scale human intuition has been stood on its head. It does seem that our universe is both vaster and stranger than we thought, vaster and stranger in fact than our minds can easily grasp. So what on earth are we to make of this five-ring circus, this ultimate Greatest Show on Earth? Reason and logic are clearly useful, but perhaps we also need time to allow ourselves to get used to it, to digest it properly.

But at this point our voyage has hardly begun. In later chapters this book will follow up on further implications of this first theme, the scale of things.

Chapter 2

Wonderlands

What banged?

Having voyaged up and out as far as it is possible to go, we seemed to reach something like an edge beyond which we could not see, a bit like the edge of the earth which in ancient times, we are told, mariners were afraid of falling over. This apparent edge of space-time is measured at 13.8 billion light years distance, echoing an event which happened presumably 13.8 billion years ago. On this specific date the remarkable fabric of space and time burst into being in one unimaginably rapid instant, triggering an event popularly known today as the Big Bang.

That, at any rate, is the currently favoured consensus, a consensus which has held for a good many decades and is based on plentiful evidence, consistent with the General Theory of Relativity and the so-called Standard Model of the Universe. At the same time the picture which it generates is exceedingly strange, and has indeed come under fairly intense scrutiny from physicists in recent years. Let's stop just for a moment. This entire universe, this fabric of space-time, once emerged, we are told, in virtually no time at all, in much less time than it took you to register the last word or two as you read this sentence. Then it rapidly inflated from an unimaginable submicroscopic scale to an equally unimaginable vastness. Leave aside for a moment the incomparable power of this event, if you will, and concentrate your attention for a moment on its strangeness. To know when the material world emerged is one thing, but this appears to be telling us when time itself began. It seems to be saying that time began at a certain point in time.

Other things follow. Since this birth event happened in an

extremely small space and extremely rapid instant, and since that event was followed by the colossal inflation which filled the vastness of space, we therefore pick up its echo from all directions. It's almost as if this instantaneous event didn't happen at any one place, but everywhere simultaneously. This surely multiplies our sense of strangeness.

Not surprisingly, we are torn both ways. The Standard Model of the Universe, deriving from Einstein's General Theory, is unrivalled in its colossal reach and its startling economy. To a lay enquirer the idea of a Big Bang is counter-intuitive in a quite fundamental sense. The whole project of the sciences does appear to assume a universality of cause and effect and therefore would seem to require a before and after, a pre-existing space-time in which cause and effect can function – or that at least is what our human intuition leads us to expect.

Nevertheless, despite its strangeness, the Standard Model remains justly celebrated and influential. It is the end result of a very particular historical provenance, building on a series of great leaps of the imagination which came to highly individual enquirers, often described as geniuses. The sheer originality of Isaac Newton, James Clerk Maxwell, Michael Faraday and others made possible the startlingly original insights of Albert Einstein, and this long provenance adds greatly to the authority of Einstein's vision of the universe.

Still, we are left with loose ends. The moment when the universe is said to have sprung into existence is called a singularity, a mathematical term which signals a limit beyond which calculations appear to break down. To some people this is bound to look like an open invitation to find an explanation which is less at odds with our experience. Perhaps we could say that this Big Bang model is the best we can do at this point in time. One group of physicists, indeed, have set themselves the target of replacing the Standard Model of the Universe within twenty years.

This model of reality, then, explains fundamental things with brilliant economy and at the same time brings us face to face with acute paradox. People by now are trying to puzzle out the factors which might have brought the Big Bang to the point, like a tipping point, at which this explosive instant of birth became unstoppable. This appears to assume a time before the Bang, before time is said to have begun. But the logic continues. If there is or was a previous something from which our universe emerged, this then might open up the possibility of a series of similar events calling a series of universes into being over much vaster stretches of time, an idea often referred to as a multiverse. The Big Bang, then, however awesome, might be perhaps no more than one event in a wider creation which as far as we can see might have no clearly definable edges or limits.

Whichever view is likely to prevail, logic seems to tell us that time and space either have a beginning and an end, or they are endless, but neither view really makes very good intuitive sense. Our universe appears to be rational through and through, yet this rationality appears to take us to either of two contradictory conclusions. Or perhaps we need to conclude that the universe is possibly not rational through and through after all – but that doesn't seem right either.

Tumbling in free fall

Perhaps you have found our voyage to the end of the universe really quite surprising, or inspiring, or disconcerting, or all of these at the same time, but we do have other dimensions to explore and other voyages to make. So once again, ensure that your seat belts are securely fastened.

You are invited to imagine a tumble through the different scales of the physical creation. Having arrived in our spaceship at the very outer limit of the universe, we can if we wish let ourselves tumble downwards into the scale of a supercluster of galaxies, and from there to the very much smaller scale of an individual galaxy, one of the estimated 100–200 billions scattered through space. Let's say this happens to be our own galaxy, the Milky Way. From there we then continue falling until we reach the scale of one of its billions of stars, perhaps one just like our own sun.

From there we can go on falling into the scale of our planet earth, then on down perhaps to the scale of a major earth-based ecosystem like the Amazon rainforest or the Sahara desert. From these it might take just a little while to arrive at a scale not far from our own actual size, close to the scale of many living creatures on our planet earth. At this point we maybe think we've arrived home, and we ask the captain to apply the brake, but it doesn't appear to be working, or perhaps he hasn't heard us properly, so we keep on falling. Here, as we keep on going in and down, we get the strangest feeling as we realise things around us are getting curiouser and curiouser.

On down we go, far beneath our own scale, eventually reaching the scale of the single cell, of which there are a few trillions in an average human body. Nevertheless as we keep on falling, the inside of the cell itself soon appears to be very capacious as we arrive at the scale of the countless denizens of the workaday world within the cell, giant molecules scurrying about their business. Nearby we notice the supergiant double helix of the DNA molecule stored like a chrysalis in the securely defended information library at the very heart of the cell. But presently even that molecular world seems large as we keep on tumbling, and soon we see how enormous each giant molecule really is as we zero in on, say, an enzyme, with its intricately folded, knobbly shape. Soon even its many tiny individual atoms start to come into view.

At this point, just as we think we must be getting down to the very fabric of the material universe, things start to become truly bizarre. Soon, as just a handful of atoms loom large before us, we realise that each atom does appear at first glance to consist largely of empty space. This is probably familiar as an idea to many people by now, but it may be worth pausing here to take a good look. A handful of electrons appear to be in some kind of cloud in orbit round the outside of each atom – and if we look carefully we can detect in the middle distance a small central point, the nucleus of the atom, where a number of particles are clustered, apparently herded like sheep in a pen. The matter of which our entire world is composed, the ultimate reliable solid stuff of which we ourselves are made and on which we rely every day, apparently isn't solid stuff at all, it's more of a fierce tension between immense energies somehow held in a stable balance within each atom. Matter, it now appears, is like a kind of captive energy. It's difficult, though, to find words for the immensity of the energy which it takes to hold it all together.

Still the brake doesn't seem to be functioning as we now find ourselves hurtling down through the nucleus at the centre of the atom. At this point we reach a world mightily stranger even than the world we have just come through. In this world particles in some sense only exist when they interact with other particles, so we have a picture, if we can imagine it, of 'potential' particles being continuously created and destroyed. In this world we can estimate the statistical probability of an individual particle's (or wave-function's) existence, but not know it with certainty. In certain conditions, moreover, particles can show 'superposition', that is, can appear in two states at once. Not only that, two or more particles can be 'entangled' in such a way that the act of measuring one particle can change some properties of the others, instantly and even at a distance.

All of this does appear to challenge more than just our intuitive notions of space, time and the solidity of matter. It appears to question the logical certainty of a fully determined creation.

Please note that this is no theoretical fantasy, this is the accepted standard physics of the atomic and subatomic world, underpinning much of modern technology, from mobile phones, lasers and satellites to the electron microscope and the MRI scanner.

This quantum world has also changed our picture of the depths of space, very different from an earlier picture of serene emptiness. This entire creation, it now appears, is made of wave-particles, only some of which are tied into atoms. It turns out that deep space, even in the voids where there are no atoms, swarms with wave-particles in perpetual but ephemeral interaction, in a continuing, eternal rhythm of creation and destruction. It's almost as if this creation were hovering between existence and non-existence.

Reflection: the span of reason?

The quantum world within the atom has been described as 'a surreal world from which the entire physical world somehow emerges'. The forces involved here are by now familiar but the strangeness of this world remains nevertheless very striking. In one sense we can understand it and learn to exploit it, but in another sense we don't really understand why things are this way at all. One author has called it 'beyond weird'.

But when we pause to think about it, there are in fact many aspects of the material world which we understand yet don't fully understand. Why, for example, does gravity attract matter in the way it does, apparently even at pretty impressive distances? Nowadays we can get used to the idea that gravity can express how mass curves light and indeed space and time, but why would it do that? It does appear that the idea of understanding something can itself be ambiguous – it is evidently not always like an on-off switch.

Summing up, we have explored the exotic world of the atom, then the exceedingly strange quantum world deep within the atom. At this point we might wonder what might perhaps lie at still deeper levels within the quantum world, and what worlds might lie deep within that in turn, and so on. There is logically no point at which we must stop, but the further we move from the familiar world we inhabit, the less it seems to mean to us.

Meanwhile in the singularity of the Big Bang we discovered an event with which human imagination likewise struggles to find meaning. These two examples, remember, the world deep within the quantum world and the dimensions beyond the Big Bang, may be connected – this vast universe, we are told, once emerged from an unimaginably tiny scale. Human reason has been successful in working much of this out, and this is a huge achievement, but its strangeness is nevertheless overwhelming. Both worlds, the world within the atom, from which the material world in some sense arises, and the event from which the material world of space-time originally emerged, both worlds are wonderfully strange.

Apart from anything else, at the extremes of the exceedingly tiny and the exceedingly vast it can become harder and harder to find anything which could serve as robust evidence. In these circumstances research sometimes tends to fall back on the ingenuity, elegance and economy of mathematical models.

For quite a few decades now some have been attempting to make sense of a world far beneath even the quantum scale, applying mathematical logic to string theory, quantum loops and other ideas which, they hope, might one day unite the extremely large and the extremely small in one single model, sometimes referred to as a Theory of Everything. People can be lyrical about the elegant mathematics of some theoretical models. Will this act as a spur to further effort, or will the difficulty of finding adequate evidence prove to be a fatal weakness in the long run? Perhaps our understanding of what counts as robust evidence will change over time. We must wait and see.

But again we come back to the same question – where do we stop? Some theoreticians in the 20th century determined a standard limit in scientific practice for ultimate smallness, set at

10^{-35} metres. This, they concluded, was the limit beyond which any calculations of size and distance simply break down and, as someone put it, 'quantum indeterminacy becomes absolute'. One author has said that at any point smaller than this the concepts of time and space no longer apply. Can that possibly mean that it is in practice inaccessible to human reason? Could we refer to this as an inner limit, an inner frontier of physical reality?

This ultimate limit is named Planck length, in honour of Max Planck, the German physicist who established the ultimate granular or quantum nature of the world within the atom. Planck length is related, incidentally, to Planck time and Planck mass, and there is also a Planck era, the name given to the period of time at or very soon after the origin of this universe. Again, all of these apparently set a scale limit to any physical reality which is open to rational investigation.

The problem is that human reason itself does not appear to have any equivalent limit. It does appear to us to be unbounded, at least in the sense that it does not reveal to us any purely logical limit to itself. Our instinct is to follow the path of reason and observation wherever it may lead us. (A later chapter will pick up this theme again.)

It is widely accepted that Albert Einstein did more than anyone else to set the shape of the modern universe in one single fabric of matter, energy, space and time. But it is Einstein's senior colleague Max Planck who gave us the other half of the picture, a quantum world, which, however tiny, is ultimately granular. Einstein became world famous. Planck is honoured in the scientific world, and celebrated especially in his own country, Germany, but beyond that is not widely known.

The framework of our modern universe, then, was given to us in the early years of the 20th century by a handful of people from different countries, among them two German physicists who knew each other well, Einstein and Planck. Each laid out a vision which was in the end triumphant. Together they define the framework of the universe we know today. But a full century later we are still trying to bring these two visions together. For there are loose ends between them. Some would say they contradict each other.

Theme 2

Frontiers of reality?

Chapter 3

Reports from the edge

Known unknowns

Astrophysicists tell us that we probably understand 4.6% of the universe. By that I think they mean 4.6% just of the astrophysics. We have some understanding of matter, light and other energy waves, of the interaction of space-time, matter and gravity, and of the forces which hold the atomic structure of matter in place. By any standards these are epic achievements. But some of the time the mathematics doesn't add up unless we assume other phenomena or forces about which we do not as yet understand very much, which we refer to as dark matter and dark energy. Dark matter, we are told, makes up something like 26.8% of the universe, and dark energy a much larger 68.6%. These figures look rather precise, but I suspect they probably conceal the profundity of what we don't yet know. As I write this, neither dark matter nor dark energy have been observed directly, although currently there is a sense of excitement about the possibility of new insights and discoveries.

The existence of dark matter is inferred because measurements of the motion and shape of stars, galaxies and galaxy clusters in gravitational response to their own contents and that of their neighbours doesn't match up with the mass, speed and distance of the detectable matter involved. It matches up only when we assume the presence of other forces or phenomena which we have not yet observed directly. (Recently astronomers have even discovered a number of so-called dark galaxies, galaxies with a massive gravitational momentum yet very few visible stars.) Most experts work on the assumption that this extra something consists of some kinds of particles, and if it does, dark matter is thought to be 84.5% of the universe's total mass of matter, meaning that the matter we can see, the matter which emits detectable waves like light, takes up only 15.5% of the matter in this universe. At first sight this looks like a pretty massive degree of uncertainty, exemplified perhaps in the very provisional sounding name 'dark matter'.

During the past few decades some observers began to say that progress in this and related fields had been disappointingly meagre, but just a few years can sometimes make a major difference. Astronomers in more recent years had been hopeful of discovering actual evidence of telltale gravity distortions picked up by ever more massively powerful telescopes, and these hopes were indeed raised in September 2015 when the first gravitational waves were recorded. Suddenly people were talking about a new era in astronomy. Such are the vagaries of scientific progress.

Dark energy is quite distinct from dark matter, despite the similarity of the two names. Evidence has been accumulating that the whole universe is expanding, perhaps partly in inertial continuation of the massive expansion following the Big Bang. So the galaxies are receding from us, apparently at an accelerating rate, but again the maths doesn't add up unless we assume that an unknown factor or factors are driving this. To some observers this might sound like a kind of negative gravity.

Again, however, there may be other explanations. It may turn out that our perception of a rapidly expanding universe is influenced by the way in which great masses of matter in galaxy clusters curve and distort the light passing through them, whereas great voids between the clusters may refract light in quite different ways. A few think that this might eventually abolish the need for a hypothesis like dark energy altogether. If the maths works out, they may even possibly conclude that the universe isn't expanding anything like as fast as people once thought. Here too there is a sense of excitement abroad, an expectation of new breakthroughs up ahead.

Another area where major discovery is now being predicted is the pattern of microwave background signals, which may be reflecting back to us echoes from the birth of our universe. Maps of the very early universe, just after the Big Bang, are being drawn up. Within the next few years further theoretical analysis of this data may yet change the way we understand how the fabric of all things sprang into existence, how it then developed, and how it continues to evolve over time.

Presumably the universe has continued to expand during the 13.8 billion years it took the microwave signals to reach us. Taking this extra expansion into account, some people now estimate that the whole thing might be as much as 46 billion light years from end to end!

Bottomless pits

Dark matter and dark energy are interesting theoretical ideas, but perhaps a bit like elusive ghosts. Black holes, by contrast, are alarmingly real, and menacingly active in their own galactic locality. It is, again, hard to see black holes directly – some would say it is by definition impossible – but we certainly can observe the dramatic effects which they exert on their immediate surroundings. A black hole forms when matter comes together which is of a sufficient gravitational mass to pull in everything around it, and as the mass grows its gravity becomes so strong that even light is pulled in – which is presumably why we can't see it.

This phenomenon was first predicted back in the late 18th century, but its importance became clearer once Einstein's new model of the universe came to be accepted. It is said that Einstein himself tried very hard to find evidence that black holes could not exist in practice, some countervailing force which would balance the extreme effects of gravity. In the end, however, the evidence for black holes accumulated.

Einstein's misgivings are understandable – black holes are

certainly weird as well as wild and violent. In the words of a recent press report, here space-time can curl up like a magician's cloak round substantial, massive objects and vanish them from the universe. In a black hole, moreover, space and time as we know them appear to come to an end.

They are also highly dramatic. Any material objects close to a black hole, not only planets but objects with the magnitude of stars, circle rapidly around it like comets, swinging in close and then arching away, accelerating sharply as they come ever closer with every circuit they make. Finally if they come too close, their matter is stretched, then shredded bit by bit and finally sucked into the dark void. This process can take some time, and as the matter stretches like spaghetti it often glows with a particularly fierce brightness. Eventually, though, this brilliant light is extinguished, sucked in beyond the so-called 'event horizon' along with everything else.

The search to capture evidence of some of the larger specimens on camera, so-called supermassive black holes, for a time focussed attention on two in particular, Sagittarius A* (pronounced 'A-star'), which sits close to the centre of our own galaxy some 25 thousand light years distant from us, and a much more active one in a galaxy named M87, in the Virgo cluster of galaxies some 50 million light years away (i.e. still relatively close to us). This search involves cooperation between major telescopes on different continents, and NASA's Nuclear Spectroscopic Telescope Array, aka NuSTAR, a satellite observatory in earth orbit. It is now thought that black holes are in fact more common than we once believed, and that there may in fact be thousands of black holes of varying sizes in a typical galaxy.

In one sense black holes are by now an accepted part of our reality. The phrase has entered the common parlance of our language. In a deeper sense, though, they remain a baffling mystery. The widely accepted mathematical model of physics, which sums up what we know of the universe, appears to stop short at the so-called event horizon of every black hole. Does time itself really stop, and does space really disappear along with the matter and light? Just like the Big Bang from which our entire universe apparently emerged, the study of black holes appears to be on the very frontier of current understanding.

It's as if the matter in this universe has different forms, depending on the degree of gravity it is subjected to. First there is matter as we know it, including solid, liquid and gas (as well as plasma). Then at sufficient mass this matter can ignite to form the nuclear fires we know as stars, which constitute most of the visible universe. When a star collapses at the end of its life cycle, or when matter collides with sufficient combined mass, the gravitational pull can in some cases be strong enough to form a black hole. So it appears that we have matter, nuclear fire, and black holes.

Current study in this field is exciting, and not just because of its sheer drama. Some people consider that a growing understanding of black holes may in time throw more light on the evolution and origin of galaxies, or even of the entire universe. One writer calls them 'gravity's engines'. Could it be that black holes in some way helped to set some of these galaxies spinning? Could some force, some engine like this have brought our universe to being, in some way similar to that other, much vaster singularity, the original bang itself? Some day in the not too distant future, who knows, we may yet achieve a better grasp of this. At all events the fabric of space, time, matter and energy is apparently pockmarked with holes, in which space-time appears to be consumed by gravity.

Soon we may understand more about the world inside a black hole, on the far side of its event horizon. Work on this is associated with the late Stephen Hawking among others. It has already become clear that black holes emit particles at certain wavelengths. Work is being done on temperature inside the event horizon. Is seems possible that over long stretches of time black holes may reduce in volume, or even peter out, a bit like a balloon. Little by little the mystery of the black hole may be opening up.

Certainly in black holes we are contemplating immense forces which toy with stars and star clusters, twist them, shred them, and then devour them. They have been called the hungry monsters of deep space. In fact their violent energy makes the nuclear fires of stars look decorous by comparison.

A Goldilocks puzzle

Some theorists believe that in our universe certain fundamental constants, like gravity, may have been set at a very precise and particular numerical value. If just one of these had been set differently, it is thought, a universe like this one might not have come into being.

What caused these dials, as it were, to be set at these particular levels? What might be the possible preconditions leading to a Big Bang? Could it be that a Big Bang is best seen as a generic term, an event which is liable to happen every so often, every few tens of billions of years perhaps, given a set of preconditions, rather than a unique never-to-be-repeated event. Might there be other universes from which Big Bangs can arise, or even universes generating further universes in something people now refer to as a multiverse? Perhaps the Big Bang led to the creation of a number of island universes, ours being just one of these. Perhaps.

As part of this scenario our own universe, indeed, might turn out to be very unusual. Perhaps events like Big Bangs might only very rarely result in a stable material space-time creation such as ours. Our universe, in fact, has been called a Goldilocks universe, that is, the fundamental forces which were generated in its Big Bang are set not too high and not too low, but just right to produce a universe like this one. Might there have been other occasions in which these forces completely failed to come together, or came together but made other universes, universes with very different, perhaps unimaginable dimensions or qualities?

So perhaps our own universe began 13.8 billion years ago, creating space-time and energy-matter in an infinitesimal moment, but perhaps this Big Bang which was part of this was more of a phase change (some people call it a Big Bounce) creating this universe out of coinciding forces in a preceding – what should we call it? – pre-universe?

It would be rather satisfying if it turned out that our present universe, having started with a stupendous bang, were to end with an equally stupendous gravitational crunch. There would be a pleasing symmetry about this, but the current evidence, such as it is, seems to be pointing in another direction. This universe, it seems, will just carry on expanding, with no time limit and no force capable of stopping it, fading steadily into – what should we call it? – nothingness? This would presumably mean that our universe once had a beginning, but in some sense or other might not have an ending. Or conceivably it might lead to another Big Bang, the birth of another universe – who knows?

Reflection: the logic of discovery?

The universe we know today, then, is at one and the same time both rational and strange. Instinctively we apply reason to understanding our world, and much of the time this does respond impressively well – and it's easy to forget how remarkable this fact is. Our universe is indeed accessible to reason, you could say friendly to reason. Yet sooner or later reason comes up against its own limits, for example when it is applied to the unimaginably large or the unimaginably small. Yet human reason is a logical system which is not self-limiting; there is no arbitrary point at which it has to stop. How do we get round a paradox like this? Perhaps we need to stop looking at reason as part of the fabric of the universe, and see it more as a feature of the natural world in us, part of our own evolutionary inheritance.

In his time Isaac Newton perhaps did more than anyone else to raise confidence that the universe was indeed splendidly rational. In a time before the great mysteries of chemistry and of living things had been uncovered, and before the vast scale of the universe had become evident, the idea eventually caught on that this creation must be fully determined, a closed system like a clockwork machine, conceived, some said, by a master designer. It was therefore only a matter of time before we would be able to explain it fully. Once we had arrived at that goal, then, the project of the sciences would presumably be complete and it would come to a natural end.

This model of a creation on a broadly human scale may have been convincing in its own time but the progressive opening up of the universe which followed, especially in the last half-century, is unavoidably transforming how we understand our reality. For a growing number of people, a human scale clockwork universe, it seems, is no longer on the agenda. The logic of discovery has changed what we see.

As the sciences continue to uncover more and more of this universe, something else typically happens. Time after time as we open up new areas of understanding we also open up whole vistas of new complexities and new questions.

One good example of this in recent years was the study of the genome, which initially aroused high hopes of finally understanding the nature of life itself. Impressive and indeed revolutionary progress has been made in many fields within genomics – leading to the impressive achievement of gene editing, for example. Developments like these transform our understanding of the immensely detailed processes of evolution at molecular level, and of the often exceedingly subtle and complex ways in which the genome interacts with its own organism, its own internal environment. At the same time another result of this progress is that we now understand much better just how far we are from coming to the bottom of things in the way we had originally hoped to do.

In the same way the recent evidence of gravitational waves, set in train by tracking the collision of two black holes, promises to open up a whole new dimension of astronomical investigation, and this will include a whole new level of questions, opening up a new field of study. Similarly recent advances in brain research, especially with the arrival of real-time mapping of brain activity, at first seemed to promise rapid advances in solving the puzzle of consciousness. Again, this has thrown up whole new landscapes of complexity. Even after so much discovery and so many breakthroughs in understanding, the ultimate enigma of consciousness remains for now unexplained.

Of course none of this rules out the possibility of major, groundbreaking advances in any of these fields in the future. Scientific investigation will always be capable of springing surprises. When we come to think of it, however, experiences like these probably describe a universal process in all human learning, not just in the sciences. When we begin to learn about a new field we often experience an exhilarating early rise in confidence. It is often only at a later point that we begin to understand how much there is still to learn, sometimes making us more thoughtful in our predictions. Our earlier confidence can then seem to us somewhat premature and even naïve. This does seem to describe the very shape of human learning.

It is tempting to think that one day perhaps far in the future the sciences will be for all practical purposes completed, the main questions essentially answered. If that were to happen, then perhaps they might then lose public interest and financial support. But since science will always remain an open-ended quest in a deeply complex universe, it does seem likely that it will carry on making unexpected discoveries and conjuring new surprises for quite some time yet.

Chapter 4

The cresting wave of time

The dreams of others

My daughter, when she was still very little, once said to me that if Mummy had met another man, she would have had a different daddy. Perhaps I should have said, 'Yes, dear,' and left it at that, but I didn't. I said, 'No, dear, that wouldn't have been you.' She looked at me with a puzzled frown, the moment passed and I think we had narrowly missed one of life's deeper questions. Of course I could also have said that if Mummy and I had conceived a baby a week before, or even five minutes before, that too would have been somebody else.

You could say in fact that each of us was selected for life, selected in a one-in-a-zillion lottery. Mum's starter pack carries a chromosomal mix which is unique and different from every single other one. The same is true for Dad's contribution(s), only there are many millions of them in a race which only one of them can win. Of course we do understand this, but at the same time it is so puzzling that we hardly ever take the logic any further.

But we know that the lottery doesn't stop there – beyond that we are a result of chance meetings between parents-to-be, sometimes unlikely meetings, sparking a mix of attraction and hesitation, only partly conscious, perhaps leading to a whirlwind, bringing into play the endless complexity of two human minds in one of the great, magical dramas of life. Beyond even that, many of us sometimes wonder about the life choices we didn't take, the paths we didn't go down. Perhaps we attended a job interview where we came second, perhaps we wondered whether to move abroad or to another part of the country. Occasions like that sometimes hang on a thread.

We could so easily have taken a different road, opening up an entirely different course of life, meeting different people (and perhaps conceiving different people).

All this is equally true going back in time as we double the ancestral actors for every generation – four for two generations back, 32 for five generations back, 1,024 for ten generations back. The fact is we are the product of great crowds of ancestors, and in each generation, each betrothal or each seized moment, the same odds apply, the same chance meetings, the same imponderable weighing of pros and cons, perhaps once in a while a fateful snap decision. In a startlingly literal sense, we really are the stuff of dreams, often the most secret and heartfelt dreams, of a host of other people. Yes, strange to say, we who live were selected for life, and this was but a small part of an immense open-ended process of natural selection, presumably stretching right back to the first living creatures on this planet.

The universe is endlessly vast and complex, and going forward in time, often bafflingly open-ended and unpredictable. Add up the endless forks in this long road, in fact, and the numbers might appear to be infinite. And we are products of the same logic and the same environment, similarly complex and similarly unpredictable, as we too are taken forward in time. (The next chapter will revisit the question of vast numbers and infinity.)

Like a great river flowing

Augustine of Hippo, in the late Roman world, arrived at the conclusion that his Creator had not made the world within a pre-existing framework of time and space, as the poem in the Book of Genesis had imagined, but had created time and space, and the world within it, all in one stupendous creative act. Many centuries later physicists assure us that time did indeed have a beginning, an explosive birth moment in which a material universe sprang into being, and with it the extraordinary phenomenon of time.

History is one way in which we try to understand the great mystery of time, but often it misleads us. History is frequently presented as a series of stories telling us about things which happened in another world called the past. This caused this and was then followed by that and it all ended up, apparently inevitably, in this or that climax. Historical accounts often seek to explain the past, to make it all simpler and easier to understand. Looking back with the benefit of hindsight it can all seem rather cut and dried. In reality, however, human affairs presumably share the same deep complexity and unpredictability as the entire physical universe.

It's not really surprising, then, that a backward-looking account of a series of events is often quite, quite different from how it felt to the people involved in these events at the time. For them, like us, it was all happening in their own experience of the present moment, so they may not have seen any more than hints of what was coming next. (One of the troubles with war, someone once said, is the consequences which were unforeseen and unintended.) In this fiendishly complex world the protagonists, even the big fish in the story, are often too preoccupied with their own immediate experience to even glance ahead. For one historian, ruminating on the sensational collapse of the western Roman Empire, it's as if the main protagonists in the story were walking backwards into the future.

For us, too, time is so close to our everyday experience that it is easy to take it for granted and forget just how very strange it all is. Pause for a moment, if you will, as you consider this next sentence.

Each moment in time is unique and will never be repeated. In the eons of time during which this universe has been in existence, each moment is unique and will never be repeated.

We cast around for comparisons to help us to describe this. Sometimes we picture it like an arrow, moving through space (in one direction only), although we know perfectly well that the arrow of time doesn't actually move at all. On the contrary, it seems to be the one thing that remains perfectly still while everything else jostles around it in ceaseless motion.

Yet the understanding of space-time in the theory of relativity can lead us to quite different conclusions. We are told, for example, that when approaching a large massive object like a star or large planet, time slows down, if only by a little. More dramatically, if we ever could hurtle across space at speeds approaching the speed of light, let's say when approaching a black hole, time inside our space pod would slow down very much more. So perhaps we could embark on a 100-year round trip, say, and then on arriving back home we would step out into a future world, like Rip Van Winkle, feeling that our journey has taken just a few hours, our clock (and our stomach) telling us it was probably about time for lunch.

Again, some physicists who write about subatomic particles do seem to be describing a strange world, saying for example that the positron is like an electron going backwards in time. The thing is, time in these examples is seen as a factor in an equation. So, is the human experience of time uniquely real, more than these theoretical models, or is it just one view among others, or maybe even some kind of delusion?

And yet despite all this there is one sense in which our human experience of time is hard and immovable. Despite the logic of theoretical physics, or for that matter the allure of science fiction fantasies (and one or two quite good films), actually travelling backwards and forwards through time in reality makes no sense at all. Likewise you cannot step outside of it, except perhaps in a dream. Time is inexorable. In practice we are locked into time.

So, take a deep breath and then consider and digest the sheer scale of the whole thing. Consider the 13.8 billion years since the birth of all things, the 10 billion years since the formation of our own galaxy, and the four and a half billion years since the birth of our solar system in one insignificant corner of our galaxy. Then consider the three and three-quarter billion years since the emergence of the earliest single-celled living systems on this earth. Compare this with the mere 500–600 million years or so since the emergence of multi-celled living creatures, the whole panoply of life on earth as we normally understand it. Finally consider the much shorter time span of modern humans, Homo sapiens, somewhere around two hundred thousand years, and the very much shorter span of the last ten thousand years or so in which historical culture has finally emerged. Take a moment of time just to contemplate the majesty and the sweep of the whole thing, carried along in the great river of time.

Reflection: the experience of time and change

Seen against this scale our sheer insignificance appears startling. Yet when we consider an individual human life from the inside, as it were, with all its narrative dynamic, its hope and its potential, its timescale can seem generous – 31 thousand days, for example, (that's very nearly 85 years) can seem an ample supply, can it not? We live our lives enclosed in a bubble of time, it seems, a world which functions perfectly well on its own scale, apparently unaffected by the awesome scale of its surroundings.

In the end, though, even on this perfectly familiar everyday level, the sheer strangeness of time can still baffle us, if we stop to think. Consider our experience of past and future, and in between them the present moment, a line which appears to have no thickness, like a line in Euclidean geometry. On one side is the past, an unrecoverable world from which we carry memory, a system of brain coding which is rational yet partial, highly creative yet not always entirely reliable. The future, on the other side, although often to a limited degree predictable, is in detail equally unreachable. So we humans seem to be carried along on a wave forever cresting into the future, an eternal moment of now, forever transforming the future into the past, that is to say, creating one unreachable world out of another. The strangeness of this can sometimes hit us suddenly. Try reflecting for a moment after you have read the following sentence.

The end of this sentence you are now reading still lies in the mists of the future, but its beginning has meanwhile started to fade into the lost realm of the past.

Recent neuroscience has added distinctive insights to this. The brain, apparently, responds to outside stimuli in milliseconds. Perfectly trivial everyday situations can seem to us instantaneous, for example when we decide to have a biscuit with our coffee. But live brain scans show that our brain has registered the decision a few milliseconds before we became aware of it. This means that our impression of making this decision consciously and in an instant appears to be mistaken on both counts. Our unconscious brain has apparently logged the decision on our behalf, and gets round to informing us a few milliseconds later.

It may be tempting to conclude, once again, that our experience of time is a delusion, but perhaps it would make better sense to see all of these pictures as real in their own context, the neuroscience, the experience and the astrophysics.

Further evidence from neuroscience indicates that our sense of the 'moment of now' is in working practice two to three seconds long. Our brain, that is, recognises an event as happening now if it is within one second or more before or after this timeline. Meanwhile on yet another level, our sense of continuity and time passing is presented to our conscious mind on a somewhat longer timescale, in practice about thirty seconds. When we come to think of it, this is also echoed in longer-term patterns. Each time of the day, for example – morning, noon, afternoon and evening – feels different to us as the flow of interior chemistry changes, bringing to each part of the day its own distinctive emotions and reactions.

Recently three scientists won a Nobel prize for discovering the biochemical mechanisms behind this sense of the rhythms of each day and night. It's hard to decide which is the more astounding, the fact that very similar chemical mechanisms like this one operate in all species of life, from algae and plants to insects and humans? Or the fact that all this, for all the species of life, is a matter of chemistry working at molecular level?

Yet as we habitually rush on past the present moment of time in the pursuit of one goal or another, it can even occasionally feel as if we are perhaps running from it, even in some discomfort with it, perhaps because we can't understand it. And yet at other times, if we give this present moment more of our attention, if we savour it and appreciate its fullness, the passage of time can restore a balance within us. Sometimes time can be a healer.

But although mentally we can keep time and space apart, we know that in reality they are woven together. All we need to do is look out into the night sky, where through the medium of light we are given the peculiar privilege of looking back in time.

Or we can cast our minds forward, quite a way forward in astronomical time. In a few billion years from now, we are told, our sun will reach the final stage of its natural life cycle. At that time it will start to grow in size, becoming what is referred to as a red giant, devouring its accompanying planets one by one, including the earth. Sometime after that it may then very likely explode, seeding its surrounding space with the material elements necessary to build future worlds.

At moments like this we can face the awesome grandeur of the whole thing. In time all things evolve, including us and all living things, but also including planets, stars, galaxies, our entire universe, all in their own way continuously evolving. Time, then, is the medium of this universal evolution, and this evolution is the natural and universal outcome of time.

Chapter 5

The measure of things

Deep complexity

The number of atoms and molecules in every cubic centimetre of the air we breathe is simply unimaginable, and this is in no sense exceptional – exceedingly large numbers are everywhere in our universe. But it's not even the totted up numbers of entities which in the end impress us most of all; it's the apparently endless ways in which the phenomena of the material world interact which lie behind the modern concept of deep complexity.

In the 19th century those working on the physics of heat realised just how very, very complex a random world of continuously moving parts must be. But it was not until the mid-twentieth century that really significant attention was paid, with the emergence of what came to be called chaos theory, to the truly awesome complexity of our creation. When chaos theory arrived it met with some resistance – people at first were reluctant to regard it as real science. Yet the dawning realisation that the universe was truly impenetrably complex through and through was potentially as groundbreaking as the earlier rise in confidence, in the 17th century, that it was rational through and through.

As soon as this deep complexity was recognised, examples sprang to mind from a wide variety of human experience. Predicting the timing and placing of earthquakes and volcanic eruptions had always been a puzzle. Worldwide weather forecasting could be at times similarly hard to predict in detail. Yet progress in studying both of these phenomena did in time yield an understanding of elements of pattern within an apparently pattern-less chaos.

The realisation soon dawned that deep complexity was not always completely random, that patterns of regularity could sometimes emerge naturally within it, especially near the borderline between simple regular behaviour and increasing complexity. Patterns of simplicity seemed to be enmeshed within chaotic complexity. On the other hand, mechanisms which were initially simple could very quickly develop in surprising and quite unpredictable directions. Tiny, apparently insignificant changes in initial conditions could lead to major changes in end results, even after just a few stages in running the model. Apparently insignificant factors could interact in ways which could quite quickly build up a disproportionate dynamic, changing the end result.

There was some speculation that this might originate in the unpredictable nature of the quantum world within the atom itself, something built into the very fabric of the material world. However you explain it, everywhere you looked there appeared to be a mix of regularity and chaos, simplicity and deep complexity. This seemed to describe the material universe at a quite fundamental level.

One image for a while captured the imagination of the public – the image of a butterfly flapping its wings on the shore of one continent, eventually in some way leading to a weather change thousands of miles away on another continent. But this image was no fantasy, especially on continents visited regularly by hurricanes, which often appeared to arise from insignificant starting conditions and whose tracks were often apparently whimsical and hard to predict in detail.

A major 'eureka' moment came with the realisation that this partly predictable and partly chaotic behaviour is highly characteristic of all human enquiry and understanding. The example of the notoriously unpredictable behaviour of stock exchanges came to mind, and likewise the dynamics of electoral behaviour and the mysterious comings and goings of consumer fashion. Even the whole debate about free will began to take on a new light. Perhaps most strikingly, however, this would throw an interesting light on to the whole enterprise of scientific enquiry itself.

A further example was the apparently random nature of the catastrophic events which have periodically menaced the very existence of life on this earth, whether caused by impacts from space or by volcanic movements deep within the earth. Volcanic events, as we have seen, are virtually impossible to predict in any detail. Yet the awesome power of some historic eruptions make today's run of the mill earthquakes look small. The eruption of Toba in Sumatra, around 50 thousand years ago, makes the much better known and more recent eruption of Krakatoa in Java look quite unimpressive. Yet even Toba is small in comparison to much earlier events.

The most recent major extinction event, which seems to have finally finished off most of the dinosaurs, was probably triggered by an asteroid estimated at more than 6 miles wide, hitting the earth off the Caribbean shoreline of what is now southern Mexico, about 65 million years ago. This impact may then have set in train a whole series of large-scale volcanic events, in turn bringing about serious climate disruption apparently lasting many thousands of years.

An event like this is simply impossible to predict in detail. Even with the high precision of today's instruments, and even taking into account the modern understanding of asteroid trajectories, it is in practice exceedingly hard to predict impact point, angle of approach, likely extent of damage, chances of the giant missile partially breaking up in the atmosphere before impact, and much besides. Back then, a difference of just a few degrees in angle of approach could have sent this great rock screeching round the earth and back off into deep space, one of history's near misses. In that case the dinosaurs might not have expired so dramatically, mammals might not have inherited the earth quite so successfully, and our human ancestors might never have evolved. The universe, it does appear, is in principle both rational and yet beyond a certain level of detail profoundly unpredictable and open-ended. At that level we might say it was, yes, unknowable.

Yet at microscopic levels this unknowability carries on. Look down a powerful enough microscope and you will see that atoms and molecules are in constant, apparently erratic, zigzag motion, related to temperature and electrostatic interaction between them. There again, observe spores or grains of dust floating in water, in constant so-called Brownian motion. Deep below this, at the level of the quantum world within every atom, there appears likewise to be continuous motion underway. The foundation of our entire physical universe, indeed, appears to be a seething mass of randomly interacting particles.

So the early scientific faith that the material world was in principle fully determined has in more recent times been significantly qualified and nuanced. It is indeed in part determined and magnificently accessible to human reason, but equally in its pervasive detail it is chaotically unpredictable and apparently unknowable. It does seem to be both of these at the same time. It's as if order and simplicity are embedded in the stark complexity of things, and can emerge given the right conditions. This may, indeed, have played a role in the evolution of a living world, as we shall see later in the book.

The logic of numbers

In all this where can we look for certainty? Mathematics, we often think, is an ultimately reliable expression of logic and reason. Arithmetic, for example, which we easily conflate with mathematics, does seem to be one hundred per cent reliable – two plus two cannot equal anything but four. Mathematics can establish a way of understanding something, can add detail and precision to it, and has the unique power to sum up an exceedingly complex situation succinctly. All of this can go far to create a sense of reality.

But despite its appearance of clarity and even finality, mathematics can so easily be misapplied, and this is indeed quite a widespread problem in public life. Governments, for example, often seem keen to measure everything that can be measured, drawing attention away from often vital things which are harder to measure. A teacher's magnetic ability to convey an infectious enthusiasm for her subject, for example, or her understanding of the learning difficulties of each highly individual character in her class – these are at the heart of high quality teaching and learning, but because they are hard to measure, they often go unnoticed – certainly by many politicians, with their league tables and statistical summaries.

Mathematical figures, moreover, do need to be interpreted. This is why statistics, as it is often said, can 'prove' almost anything you like. If 25 per cent of survey respondents support some proposal, for example, although you cannot honestly make this mean 75 per cent, you can present it as 'only a meagre 25 per cent', or as 'as much as 25 per cent'.

Besides, this promise of certainty can be seductive, and can lead us to surprising conclusions. For example, the mathematics of some problems in physics may work better if we assume, say, three extra spatial dimensions, dimensions we cannot actually sense. In a case like this it is tempting to conclude that these dimensions must be real – because the numbers do add up. But what status could we give to these new dimensions? In what sense can they be said to be 'really out there'?

Mathematics is, in the end, a system of pure logic which, strange to say, is in some sense independent of the human experience of reality. The great mathematician Kurt Gödel claimed he had proved that in physics, any mathematically-based theory will always be incomplete, despite its apparent precision. Could it be that we respect it because it satisfies our hunger for simplicity in this massively complex universe?

Quite apart from all this, numbers can in any case be powerfully counter-intuitive. You may have heard the (allegedly Chinese) tale of the peasant who begged the Emperor to give him one single grain of rice, and for every square on the Emperor's gaming board all he had to do was to double the number. The Emperor later regretted agreeing to this at first quite amusing request – in the end there were simply not enough grains of rice in all the Empire's granaries to meet it.

Imagine a ten by ten board, similar to a chess board. By the fifth square the peasant has 16 grains of rice, and by the end of the first line of ten squares he has 512 grains, a perhaps slightly surprising sum, but not unreasonable, not too far removed from what one might intuitively expect. By the end of the second row, however, the peasant has amassed 524,288 grains, and by the end of the third row more than 500 million grains. Just one more square, the first one in the fourth row, brings in well over a billion grains of rice.

This might strike us intuitively as really quite surprising, but at this point as we keep on doubling from square to square, something happens which is both bizarre and highly significant – in just two or three squares the numbers become stratospheric, and then very quickly after that they become simply unimaginable – and we're not even halfway across our ten by ten gaming board.

Simple sequential doubling is powerful, using the power base two, but using the power base ten is clearly going to be very much more powerful. If we then use the metre as a standard for measuring distance, then a kilometre, a thousand metres, is 10 to the power 3 (conventionally written 10^{3m}) and a thousand kilometres (i.e. a million metres) 10^{6m}. The circumference of the earth, as it happens, is approximately 40,000 kilometres – almost halfway between 10^{7m} and 10^{8m}.

It is, of course, very convenient to have such an impressively succinct and powerful notation system in a universe in which things do often come in billions and trillions. By following the logic of numbers, it seems, we can in some way pin down this vast universe, and thereby achieve a kind of understanding of it.

Let's keep going. The distance from the earth to the sun is close to 150 million kilometres, or somewhere over 10^{11} metres. It so happens that a single light hour, the distance light travels in an hour, is just a bit more than a billion kilometres, close to 10^{12} metres. A light year is not far off ten thousand light hours, so a single light year is close to 10^{16} metres. Many of the stars we can see in the night sky, as far away as a thousand light years, are up to 10^{19} metres distant.

By similar calculations our home galaxy, the Milky Way, is 100 thousand light years from end to end, that is 10^{21} metres. Relatively close galaxies, at say 100 million light years distant, would then be something like 10^{24} metres away. Some of the most distant galaxies, situated out in deep space, could be in the region of, say, ten billion light years away, that is, 10^{26} metres. The estimated size of the entire observable universe, at 27.6 billion light years across, would then be some way beyond 10^{26} metres.

An important conclusion arises, perhaps surprising to some but nevertheless fundamental. These extraordinary figures, although unimaginably huge, demonstrate to us that this universe is not limitless. It is unimaginably vast, but oddly enough not infinite.

This mathematical logic applies equally to the smallest imaginable things. An unfertilised human egg, the largest cell in a human body, is around a tenth of a millimetre across, that is a ten-thousandth of a metre, conventionally expressed as 10^{-4m}. A DNA double helix, compactly folded in its place within every cell, would be around 10^{-8m}, a relatively simple atom around 10^{-10m}, and the central nucleus within that atom roughly $^{-14}$ to $^{-15m}$.

As we venture down beyond this point it becomes technically more and more difficult to measure anything with any degree of accuracy. Subject to this caveat, however, the particles known as neutrinos are thought to be between 10^{-20m} and 10^{-23m} (no doubt allowing for a significant margin of error). But how far does it make sense to carry on going down in scale? Purely logically there is no point at which we have to stop. Practically, however, physicists have drawn a line at an unimaginable 10^{-35} metres, the so-called Planck length which was mentioned in an earlier chapter.

Mathematics, then, can express the size of all things whatsoever, going up to the entire observable universe at somewhere beyond 10^{26m}, and going all the way down to Planck length at 10^{-35m}. These figures, then, do seem to tell us something about the scale of this universe. But mathematics itself, as a purely logical system, knows no such limits. Mathematicians recently chasing the largest known prime number have reached sums involving millions of digits. Powerful new generation computers are presumably pushing this even further. Try imagining 10 to the power of several billions.

Mathematical notation, being so very powerful and succinct, often has the effect of telescoping these vast scales in our minds. If the human egg measures at 10^{-4m} and the DNA double helix at 10^{-8m}, our first intuitive reaction might be to think that these two were of broadly comparable size. In fact it means that the egg is ten thousand times bigger than the DNA, a difference of four noughts. Similarly a fairly basic atom, at 10^{-10}, is in fact about a hundred times smaller than the tightly folded bundle of DNA at the heart of the cell. It is also, incidentally, a million times smaller than a human egg.

Let's visit the Emperor's ten-by-ten gaming board one more time. If we multiply by ten rather than just doubling as we move from one square to the next, it is clear that our numbers will become stratospheric much more quickly. By the end of just the first row of ten squares we would have reached 10^{10}, in other words ten billion. By the end of the second row we would have 10^{20}, and so on. By the final square at the end of the gaming board we would have 10^{100}. But this sum is quite possibly greater than the number of particles in this entire universe.

Reflection: the ultimate paradox?

This figure, 10^{100}, was arrived at through mathematical reasoning, and yet it appears at first sight to be beyond the scale of any imaginable human reality. As we have seen, the mathematics will reach no barrier, there is no point at which calculation has to stop. It may be useful to spell this out with some care. Because mathematics has no built-in stopping point, it seems at first sight to point to infinity. So once again we would do well to be wary of our human intuition. Instinctively we might imagine that infinity is somehow similar, somehow comparable to the exceedingly large numbers we have been considering. But on reflection this is surely mistaken. These numbers, although unimaginably vast, are in reality far from being infinite.

As we have seen, the observable universe is of the order of 10^{26} metres across. The number of Planck lengths in every metre, Planck lengths being the very boundary of measurable smallness, is 10^{35}. So the number of Planck lengths it would take to reach across the entire observable universe is 10^{26} times 10^{35}, or 10^{26+35}, which makes 10^{61}. These are indeed stratospheric, unimaginable numbers, but they do nevertheless provide a measure of the scale of this universe.

Now let's try to approach infinity. Let's first repeat the above calculation a further billion times, and then repeat the entire resulting operation a further billion times over. Then keep on doing this whole exercise continuously for, say, a thousand billion years. Here the dimensions of reality are being stretched and expanded to a point where they no longer refer to anything we can call a real world – but we still haven't reached infinity.

In short, no matter how long we try in this universe of ours, infinity never arrives. This, moreover, is true by definition, a matter of logic, not evidence.

Still, infinity is a logical, mathematical concept and as such it does have logical consequences. If there ever were, for example, a creation consisting of an infinite number of universes such as ours, then anything that conceivably could happen in that creation, sooner or later would happen. In an infinite creation, it is sometimes said, a monkey, typing at random on a keyboard without any comprehension of what it is doing, would eventually at some point type out perfectly the complete works of Shakespeare.

Something like this idea has featured in literature and film, and among speculative philosophers pondering human life choices, in which we can imagine apparently infinite numbers of parallel possibilities. Evidently this is a fertile idea, and we are capable of imagining truly staggering numbers, but in this real universe we still cannot arrive at infinity.

The truth, it would seem, is that infinity lies in a world of dream and imagination, an exciting world perhaps, but it cannot be part of this material universe. In other words this universe we find ourselves in can be both unimaginably vast and real, but it cannot be infinite and real.

Or so it would seem. Yet our language tends to follow our intuition and to blur the distinction between truly vast numbers and infinity. So language appears to lead us in one direction, mathematical logic in another.

More conclusions follow. We might say that no amount of 'finites' can ever add up to infinity. Reality might be unimaginably vast and impenetrably complex, but to say that reality has no limits whatever appears to make no sense. In the carefully chosen words of some theorists, this universe of ours is 'finite but unbound'.

In the end mathematics, being ultimately a matter of logic, is capable of being applied to experience, but not limited by experience. Mathematics, then, can accommodate infinity, but reality apparently cannot.

Forgive me if I pick through this just one more time. The singularity in every black hole, we are told, is 'an infinitely small point where the gravitational field is infinitely high'. Infinitely. That is what the mathematics tells us. Even more remarkably, the singularity which preceded the Big Bang at the very inception of our universe is thought to be 'of infinite gravitational density, containing within itself all the mass and space-time of the universe'. (Let's pause just for a moment in passing. This mathematical entity, this unimaginably tiny point of singularity, once contained within itself all the mass and space-time of a universe about to burst into existence. This is quite a picture – but let's move on.)

So a singularity, a mathematical concept, is expressed in an equation which requires infinity, and we do depend on mathematics to explain the reality of our universe, but infinity apparently can have no place in that reality. Just to repeat, then, we need a concept of infinity to explain our surrounding reality, but infinity is nowhere to be found in that reality. This, surely, is the ultimate paradox of infinity.

Yet in the previous chapter, when we considered the endless possibilities of diverging life choices (and if we were then to add to this already impressive sum the great sweep of the evolution of the living world), the possibilities did seem endless – tempting to call them infinite in fact. At this point, when we think about it, it may be perfectly natural to feel a bit overawed. Are we perhaps reaching the limits of language itself?

Just before we pause for breath, one final point. Short of actual infinity, the material reality of this universe does seem to have its own natural limits in any case, at dimensions which are exceedingly small, far 'beneath' or far down 'inside' the quantum world within the atom, or exceedingly vast, up and away far beyond the Big Bang, or indeed, like the whole thing, just unimaginably complex. Well beyond these frontier territories its reality in practice seems to fade away to nothing, or at least nothing that makes any kind of sense.

The picture emerging

But this universe of ours does give us a powerful jolt of reality, and this does matter to us. It's as if we are born looking for this reality, and when we find it, wherever we find it, we recognise it and welcome it. Instinctively, it seems, we know that if it makes sense, we make sense. It's like recognising a kinship with our universe, despite its wild, baffling scale, a kinship because it does make a magnificent kind of sense.

Soon we will have reached just the halfway point in this book. Ahead of us we still have whole new worlds to discover, so maybe this will be a good time to take stock. What stands out so far?

First, this universe is, we could say, fundamentally friendly to reason, and we often take this for granted, yet simplicity, pattern, law is hidden amongst the overwhelming complexity of its endless detail. The wonder is that human reason can actually discern pattern and a degree of simplicity in this picture at all.

At the same time this universe does seem to have an odd quality. New discoveries generate new questions. The more we discover, the more we realise how much there is still to discover. So this surrounding reality is always open to new discovery, and this gives it the open edge of something only partially understood. It is rational and at the same time mysterious.

Some current science writers say that all we have left are the problems we haven't yet solved, as if we already know what these problems are. But science is an open quest, and we cannot know for certain what discoveries might be around the corner. Major breakthroughs in the past have repeatedly caused surprise. Curiously, those who think we will soon crack the whole thing seem to picture an inherently limited universe which a relatively unlimited human reason will eventually master. But by now it is becoming clear that it is this universe which is unlimited – finite but unbound. Perhaps it is human reason, one of its by-products, which is surely more likely to have its own natural limits.

It's perfectly true that in some current problem areas, like dark matter or black holes, people do expect to achieve a fuller understanding at some point in the foreseeable future. In some problem areas, however, like the extremely small or the extremely large, there is a more fundamental difficulty. As we discovered in an earlier chapter, there does seem to be an upper and lower limit beyond which human reason at present comes up against barriers. Either it hits contradiction and paradox or else it appears to fade away into nothing.

Perhaps it is all too easy to underestimate the 'problems we haven't yet solved'. The thing is, we can only guess at the scale of what is left. Quite simply but perhaps profoundly, we don't know what we don't yet know.

Is there a way through this conundrum? Maybe the universe isn't simply 'all that is'. Maybe it is better defined as all that we humans can make sense of. Rationality, then, would be understood as part of what we mean by reality. This would mean that these two limits of scale, beneath the quantum world and beyond the Big Bang, may be true limits of a rational and therefore a real universe. But who knows, these two limits of scale may yet change.

Mathematics might provide a way through this puzzle. Elegant mathematics can be impressive, for some even intoxicating. Who knows, in time our ideas of what counts as evidence may yet change. Hypotheses based on increasingly sophisticated computer modelling, for example, may eventually acquire a growing credibility as part of our picture of reality, even in the absence of what we today would regard as hard evidence.

Beyond this, however, our sense of a ubiquitous apparently unfathomable complexity through all things may pose even more fundamental problems. Will we at some point come up against ultimate barriers of complexity beyond which reason cannot meaningfully reach? Once again, we can't be sure. A mere century or so ago, after all, some of the best minds had concluded that the atom was an ultimate barrier beyond which human reason couldn't reach. Science can be tantalising in its possibilities. For a deeply complex, random universe is also open-ended, ultimately hard to predict in detail, but always open to unexpected possibilities.

The physicist Carlo Rovelli sums up the exuberance and zest of it all. Here is a reality, he says, in which 'universes explode, space collapses into bottomless holes, and the unbounded extensions of interstellar space ripple and sway like the surface of the sea.' We have come a long way from the staid, serene universe of Isaac Newton.

The first half of this book has revealed a universe which is rational all right but more than just rational. Being hugely complex, it is also in principle always open to new possibilities. Partially unknown and unpredictable, it can spring surprises. Always and everywhere energetic, it never ceases to create newness, freshness, youth.

And what about us? How do we fit into this? We too are rational and yet at the same time deeply complex, hard to predict yet by the same token open to unexpected possibilities, true children of our universe.

Chapter 6

A tale of origins

Full circle

The first half of this book, parts one and two, has spanned the entire creation. Part three will soon narrow the focus down to life on one small planet, the one we call home. Part four will then concentrate attention on one single species, Homo sapiens, us ourselves and our drive to understand the whole thing – like completing a circle.

This narrowing of the focus raises two questions which lie close to the heart of this book. Firstly, is the life which has colonised planet earth something bizarrely and totally unique? Or might it be the kind of thing which this universe can create every so often perfectly naturally, say every few hundred million years? Secondly, are we, Homo sapiens, with our highly distinctive, questing intelligence, likewise simply a weird exception, or are we something which our universe, in similar fashion, is liable to produce perfectly naturally every cosmic once in a while?

Many of us who grew up in the 20th century absorbed a picture of a creation which was widely accepted as ultimately rational yet had these same two great unexplained gaps in it. The existence of life was simply accepted as a wonder, an unexplained miracle. But what about us, humanity itself? Even as Darwin's ideas were coming to be accepted by more people, the idea that we humans could have evolved by stages from something prehuman was still for many people too implausible, too big a mental leap. So humanity had to be an exception, a special creation, and presumably alone in its uniqueness.

This view still, I suspect, influences unconscious assumptions today about who we are. We still sometimes assume that we were put into this world, as though from somewhere else, rather than growing out of it. This in turn has kept alive the largely unexamined assumption that we don't really belong here, that this universe has nothing to do with us. That does seem to be how it still feels for quite a number of people today. But does this view make any sense any longer? New evidence has been accumulating all the while during the last few decades. Perhaps it's time we took a closer look at it.

Common stardust

How long did it take to create this voyager gazing up at the night sky and trying to figure it all out? The basic numbers have been laid out in previous chapters, but perhaps they are worth repeating here – near enough 14 billion years since the material universe burst into existence, about 10 billion years since the galaxies formed, four and a half billion since our own sun ignited and the solar system emerged in one small corner of our home galaxy. Meanwhile it took several billions of years to fire the elements of the material world in the nuclear furnaces of the stars and then scatter them across space in sufficient density to create the molecular biochemistry of life, the ingredients of life's recipe. Almost 10 billion years, then, from the creation of all things just to the starting point of life on this planet.

The earliest versions of living matter were probably already coming together well within the first billion years of the earth's formation. (Recently-discovered fossils of single-celled creatures have been dated as far back as 4.28 billion years ago.) It then took 3–4 billion more to come up with the modern eukaryotic cell, the basis of all multi-celled life on earth today. (More of this in the next few chapters.) Ten billion years for the ingredients, then, plus three billion or more for the cellular foundations of all life, makes something in the region of thirteen billion years so far. On top of all that it took little more than half a billion years, it appears, to create you and me.

Although the molecules from which living tissue is put together are in the main highly complex, the atomic elements from which these molecules were made include principally hydrogen, nitrogen, oxygen and carbon, four of the commonest elements in existence. We also contain smaller quantities of a handful of other elements, notably potassium, sodium, calcium, phosphorus and sulphur, and smaller quantities of quite a few others.

The matter created as a direct result of the Big Bang was overwhelmingly the simplest element, hydrogen (along with some of the second simplest element, helium). The other elements, as we have seen, were essentially baked from these two original ingredients in the intense nuclear fires of the stars. Then, at the natural end of these stars, many of them exploded, spraying these elements far and wide across surrounding space. This whole cycle of creation evidently took its course at different times and locations over several billion years, seeding interstellar space with the elements of our natural world.

This process continues today – so-called supernovas, exploding stars, have been sighted in historical times in our home galaxy, the Milky Way, the latest sighting occurring in January 2014. But things are about to change. Some of the latest state-of-the-art giant telescopes, soon to come on-stream, have been designed to locate further supernovas among the countless galaxies in the far reaches of space. The designers of these machines are confident that they will make thousands of sightings every year. So although supernovas in our home galaxy are evidently pretty rare, it is also clear that in this universe taken as a whole, with its hundreds of billions of galaxies, there are likely to be very large numbers of them.

As we focus on this scene we cannot help recalling once again our own fragility and insignificance. Yet here we are, made of the same stuff. Hydrogen, as we know, is one of the two ingredients of water and therefore one of the major ingredients of life on our planet, which probably developed under water and today is water-based. Much of the hydrogen in this water base dates no doubt from that original birth event 13.8 thousand million years ago, the rest being made in stars in the subsequent intervening billions of years. That is how long it took just to make the ingredients in sufficient quantities from which life might one day develop.

This leads to an important conclusion. In order to bring forth living cells, and for that matter intelligent life forms, you probably need a universe built on this scale in space and time. So the very existence of life, and of us trying to work all this out, silently witnesses to the size and age of this creation. As it turns out, then, the instinctive shiver we might get when we contemplate our insignificance sits oddly alongside a sense of awestruck wonder that we are part of such an immense, spectacular phenomenon at all.

Equally impressive is the astonishing evolution, from initially non-living molecules, of the great buzzing panoply of life on earth. This evidently needed another few billion years, most of which was necessary to build stable, complex living cells, the basis of all life on earth today. In particular, the emergence of multi-celled life couldn't get started until a whole list of other things had been put in place. For this kind of life to develop, then, it evidently needed a further four billion years of relative peace and stability on this planet.

We are creatures built on this scale. All the elements from which we are made had their ultimate origins in the birth moment of all things some 13.8 billion years ago. Every last bit, every last constituent of this creation, after all, is insignificant when we consider it on its own, but no constituent of this creation exists on its own. Nor do we. All things whatsoever, including us, are woven together in one single fabric of matter, energy, space and time. So you could say that we too are only insignificant at first glance. When we fully understand how closely and intimately we fit into the whole thing, the picture changes. Ultimately we are exceedingly complex creations, tiny and insignificant in ourselves, but nevertheless expressing the unique glory of this unimaginable, perfectly stunning, thoroughly improbable universe.

And in recent times we have learned something else. If small is beautiful then intricate and tiny is especially beautiful, and intricate, tiny and alive much more so again. It has become simply naïve to dismiss worlds built in tiny dimensions as insignificant, as if they were deemed unworthy of our attention.

A unique exception? or a wider pattern?
How widespread in the universe is this delicate, fragile phenomenon of life? How typical is it, how naturally characteristic of the material creation? We will shortly be considering the extraordinary degree of complexity which goes to make up fully functioning, living creatures. It's tempting to say that with this degree of complexity, and the veritable forest of interconnecting preconditions necessary for it to thrive, life such as we have on planet earth surely has to be unique. This huge degree of complexity is simply too improbable to repeat itself, or so we might think.

But when we remember the extraordinary scale on which the universe is built, with its two hundred billion galaxies, it can occur to us that there may very well be many other living habitats. The logic behind this now appears to have been turned inside-out – if this kind of extraordinary phenomenon can happen once, and clearly it has, there appears to be no reason why, in a universe built on this scale, it shouldn't happen many times over. Strange to say, it seems that a truly vast universe can eventually produce vanishingly unlikely things, rare no doubt but perfectly natural.

Will other life systems be in any way similar to ours? Suppose that the quest to find life on remote exoplanets circling other stars actually succeeds, and we pick up unmistakable signs of some form of life. Even then there are only quite remote chances of finding a planet on which intelligent life has coincidentally reached a similar level to that on earth at this precise point in time. Finding evidence of living systems is one thing, but actually meeting little green men (who speak quite good English) is quite another.

Nevertheless, people in recent years have begun to think there may be some form of primitive life, or at least the biochemical prerequisites of life, actually quite widely distributed throughout interstellar space. Just in the last few years there was a flurry of excitement about evidence of complex organic molecules, confirmed after the very first landing on a comet (comet 67P/Churyumov-Gerasimenko). So the hunt for some kind of life is on, and not just in far-flung, remote locations, but at various locations in our solar neighbourhood. There is currently speculation, for example, that there might be life on Jupiter's moon Europa or on Saturn's moons Titan and Enceladus, or even on our neighbour Mars. We are told that even on Venus, whose surface calls to mind a true likeness of Hades, conditions favourable to life may exist some 70 kilometres high above the surface, where water and sunlight are in abundance and temperatures are said to be balmy. Is it even possible that life forms may exist miles down within the mantle of our own planet earth. Some experts take this seriously. There is more water stored in the mantle than in all the surface oceans on the planet.

Nor is all this just a matter of speculation. Deep in ocean trenches here on earth strange life forms have indeed been found, which draw energy from hot volcanic vents, so-called smokers, evidently well beneath depths to which sunlight can penetrate. Did this living world drift down from surface depths and adapt to a sunless existence, or is this life form truly independent in origin from ours? Recent work in the genomics of ancient single-celled creatures seems to point to a common ancestry between these two living worlds, the deep-sea world and the solar-based surface world. Other work may, however, be hinting that the very earliest flowering of life on earth may nevertheless have been deep in our oceans.

All of this is creating an expectation that life is no longer a wholly unique, isolated case, but may be a characteristic feature of the material world, rare no doubt, but perfectly natural. Given favourable conditions, it does appear that this universe can spontaneously generate life, its plentiful ingredients ready to come together at any time, like a constant waiting agenda.

Over long stretches of time living systems diversify. This means that even in the most menacing of life-threatening circumstances there is a significant chance that some of this great diversity will survive, and this can give to life as a whole an incredible capacity to evolve new forms apparently out of nothing. Life therefore has a way of digging in, even in the most unpromising environments. So although it may take a truly remarkable coming together of unlikely preconditions for life to get started, this only needs to happen on a planet such as earth on a very, very few rare occasions, or maybe indeed just once.

Evidently, then, life requires a universe built on what seems to us a simply enormous scale. Once all the endless list of prerequisite conditions have finally coincided, then living systems additionally require a very, very long period of relative stability, alternating with periods of great threat and disruption, creating a span of time in which it can adapt and survive. Conditions on this earth have been at times far from ideal. As we saw earlier, major catastrophes have occurred, in which life was all but wiped out, yet apparently insignificant remnants did survive here and there. A tiny percentage survival rate is on occasion sufficient, and given eons of time, can create new worlds.

And yet although it has lasted for billions of years, life could equally be all but extinguished in less than a thousand years, the blink of an eye in universe time. Life, it appears, is tenacious and at one and the same time perilously fragile.

There is something about that which can arouse both our admiration and our concern. Once we properly understand all this, the survival of this precious biosphere of life may in the end matter intensely to us, more than anything else. It may take a while, a good few decades in fact, but quite possibly this rise in human awareness and concern may be already underway in our century.

Theme 3

Understanding self-assembly

Chapter 7

The dance of all life

To sum up, it has taken something of the order of 500–600 million years for multi-celled life – mammals, birds, insects, fish, amphibians, reptiles, and the vast diversity of plant life – to evolve and diversify and spread around the earth. (Some estimates put it back farther than that.) Before this it took more than three billion years to develop single-celled living things like bacteria, and before that, in turn, perhaps up to a further half billion to accomplish the most baffling achievement of all, getting life underway in the first place, starting from non-living ingredients.

Students of the living world report the truly remarkable social organisation in a beehive or of an anthill for example, a degree of smoothly running complexity which can take the breath away. But these are in no sense unusual – plentiful examples of wonderful complexity can be found in abundance wherever we look in nature, notably in the development of all species from fertilised egg to mature adult. Life, it appears, is everywhere miraculous yet wholly natural.

The living cell

The fundamental building block of all multi-celled living creatures, all animals and plants, is the eukaryotic cell. There are around 35 trillion of these in a human body – perhaps a good few million in just the top half of your thumb, say. The internal working of this cell is often compared to a city state, with transport networks, manufactory assembly lines, power stations, working currency, policing systems, archive library, waste disposal, entry and exit ports and much besides.

This whole world operates with a high degree of working

efficiency at the minuscule, invisibly tiny level of complex molecules, all achieved by an immensely intricate cascade of local, sometimes surprisingly simple biochemical reactions. Astonishingly to us, the molecules appear to have no actual blueprint, no idea where they are going, they just interact with each other in unimaginably complex chains and networks.

The genome, a bit like a reference library stored in the nucleus of each cell, is sometimes thought of as being a command centre, but this is probably altogether too simple. In it is stored information vital to keeping the show on the road, coded in the biochemical language of DNA. Many times per second biochemical messengers visit it, take copies of bits of it, perhaps set up orders for them to be re-copied and sent to specific locations within the cell. In ways like this the genome interacts with a veritable blizzard of local networking. It is evidently a crucial contributor to a bafflingly complex chain of molecular events but only rarely does it directly dictate how things will be.

Quite apart from the mind-boggling wonder of all this operating at molecular level in every one of a myriad of cells throughout your body every microsecond of your life, this degree of complexity is eloquent witness to a very long, exceedingly ancient history. This level of complexity can only be the product of great stretches of evolution.

All plants and animals are at root collectives of single cells, cells whose ancestors progressively surrendered their independence and took on an increasingly specialised role within a multi-celled community. So cells today come in many specialised varieties, blood cells, brain cells, muscle, bone and cartilage cells, the cells of all the major organs and many more.

An effective currency? Adenosine triphosphate, always readily available in abundant supply throughout the cell, is a uniquely versatile molecule capable of assisting in all kinds of biochemical reactions. Like a currency, it effortlessly enables a wide range of diverse activities to be coordinated.

Transport systems? Kinesins are motor-proteins which clamber around the cell transporting a whole variety of items. To do this they presumably need some way of reading off destinations to which items are to be delivered, instructions on how to get there, and some kind of position-sensing feedback, to keep it all on track.

A typical cell also has cell reproductive systems, in which the entire cell meticulously splits in two, as well as cell-ageing and cell-suicide systems. Cell suicide systems are vital in managing the detail of body shaping and development over time, from the shape of the fingernails and toenails of a maturing, few centimetres long embryo, to the loss of hair colour in the later years of adult life.

There will be naturally occurring errors in a system like this and there will therefore have to be further systems to identify these errors in good time, and either patch a correct version or, if the error is too major, arrange for the offending item to be conveniently destroyed. An order for a replacement will then have to be issued, sent to the manufactory with some kind of tag perhaps denoting one of several levels of urgency. There again, the manufactories may at times overproduce, so they too will have to be monitored and the production rate slowed down for a while, or in emergency perhaps suddenly increased. The whole thing is everywhere continuously monitored and finely tuned, like a smoothly running racing car – all of this within a world so small that we cannot actually see it.

The living cell is so extremely tiny to our eyes that it is natural for us to think that it must be all very cramped in there. How big is a cell, relative to the nucleus and other constituents at work within it? I once had this visualised to me at a meeting in a hall which was two stories high and roughly cubic in shape. Imagine this hall, maybe 50 feet cubed, as a typical average-sized cell. Within this, I was told, the nucleus might be the size of a rather large melon, and the myriads of giant molecules travelling around going about their particular business would range in size from that of a small chocolate bar to an individual chocolate. At first sight the cell might seem quite spacious inside, but nevertheless it does get quite crowded and hectic most of the time because of the sheer numbers of constituents working away all the time, somehow managing to coordinate their activities without serious blockages.

How big would be the entire human body in which this cell lives? On this comparison it would stretch several hundred miles, perhaps the distance between London and Inverness.

From egg to embryo

As we saw in a previous chapter, each of us is a product of a one in several million chance. This moreover is true of every generation of our ancestors, going back into the mists of time, back indeed to our prehuman predecessors, our mammalian cousins, our more distantly-related vertebrate relatives, and so on. All living creatures, and every one of us, are spawned into life through a game of incalculable chance, embedded into vast stretches of time.

That's remarkable enough, but still more remarkable is the maze of biochemical reactions whereby a single fertilised cell becomes a living creature. (Hold on tight, there may be another voyage coming up.) The sperm head rapidly unloads its DNA as soon as it has arrived inside the egg, then after a variety of preliminary tasks have been completed, the sperm DNA lines up with the egg DNA, as though for a country dance, and presently zips up with it. Presumably, if this is to happen successfully time after time, there must be a biochemical agent whose job it is to guide the two chains of DNA together and give the go-ahead to start the zipping process only when they are exactly aligned. Once this is assured, the cell then duplicates everything, arranges itself into two halves, which then pull apart and pinch off, leaving two cells.

The precision of this takes the breath away, yet this is part of the everyday routine of all living systems everywhere. The first division takes about 24 hours, so by day two you are now two cells. By similar processes, three days later you are a ball of sixteen cells, a so-called morula.

By the end of week one this continuously multiplying morula is developing a fluidy space in the centre, and with this a series of chemical signals indicating an inside and an outside. The outside cells will go on to become the placenta, the inside cells morphing in time into a new person. Soon the morula (now called a blastocyst) has more cells at one end than the other, so there is not only an inside and an outside, there is now also a top and bottom and a front and back, all signalled biochemically. All this time cells are multiplying rapidly and eventually you reach the giant size of a centimetre or two. It is now a week to ten days since the champion sperm won the race to fertilise the egg.

This is just the simplest of photo-snaps of a very small part of a fiendishly complex network of processes in the earliest stages of which you and I came to be. Life is a self-assembling, naturally growing system. Over long stretches of time the harsh logic of natural selection has favoured certain kinds of complexity, and over many, many millions of years this complexity has grown exponentially. Typically this process works by means of the simplest, most local mechanism, like the difference in the developing blastocyst between top and bottom, front and back. At the same time it doesn't design a body to fit its environment. There is no mechanism which can think ahead in that way. Instead, over countless millennia, it tinkers and experiments with an accumulation of accidental little changes and add-ons. Strikingly, a natural error rate and the vagaries of pure chance are crucial to the evolution of this wonder through long, long eons of time.

Again and again natural selection produces an organism which has all the appearance of being designed in exquisite detail for its particular environment, yet this is often the end result of a bizarre, apparently aimless series of circumstances involving a crucial role for simple random chance.

Sculpted from the inside

Consider the human hand, a beautifully designed multi-purpose tool made for controlled grasping and manipulating objects, but also capable of infinitely sensitive exploration by touch. The more we examine it, the more remarkable it becomes. How, we think, does a hand 'know' when and where to split a wrist into five bones, not four and not six, and when and where to then separate these five into separate digits, when to make a row of joints, when to start making nails, and not least when to finish with the extraordinary scrolled designs at the fingertips? How does it 'know' all this?

The development of the hand, from the earliest stages in the womb, is partly guided by a system of gradients. Certain biochemical agents are present in steadily rising or falling concentrations, and this cues other sensors to respond in ways appropriate to the point at which they find themselves. This guides them how to respond in building at that point. Again this is an extreme oversimplification of a very much more complex picture, but it illustrates the kind of principle on which bodily design and growth are achieved and managed in detail. So despite our instinctive way of trying to understand it and describe it, 'knowing' in the normal sense of the word doesn't come into the process at any point.

Early work in this field was done on fruit flies, whose bodies follow the insect pattern of three very clearly differentiated sections, each with appropriate appendages. Head, thorax and abdomen sprout antennae, legs, wings, eyes and so on according to where along the length of the body they are situated.

By simply changing the concentrations of these gradients, experimenters demonstrated, the gene complex governing the formation of a leg, for example, could be activated in the head or abdomen instead of the thorax. This mechanism or something like it presumably governs much of the shape and development of creatures – including insects, fungi, plants, bacteria – throughout the living world.

The hand is perhaps a good example to choose because it is graphic, familiar and apparently relatively simple. The number of features in our bodies which must be initiated and monitored in some kind of similar way must run into millions, perhaps billions. Why have I kept my hair while my brother has lost much of his with age? Why can some people eat what they like and hardly ever put on weight, while others are constantly struggling with diets? These are details which come to our attention. There are no doubt many, many more details which go entirely unnoticed. Evidently principles and mechanisms similar to this one have been in operation in the evolution of multi-celled life during the last few hundred million years on earth.

What can we say? Our words can only express a limited amount. The logic of human language focuses on one thing at a time. Evidently it cannot easily express the vivid reality of this kind of simultaneous, multitasking world.

All of life does seem to be played out in another language, the language of immensely complex molecules. We humans share these molecules or near variants of them with a huge range of other species, including not only chimpanzees and cats and dogs but also bumblebees, tree frogs and the rocket and lettuce leaves on your salad plate. This, indeed, provides dramatic evidence of the exceedingly ancient ancestry we have in common with all of life. We are, after all, made of the same molecular stuff.

The spark

What drives all this astonishing activity? Wherein lies the spark of life? What is it that distinguishes life from non-life? For centuries these were amongst the great unanswered questions, the ultimate mysteries. Then from the early 19th century onwards people began to realise that electricity was in some way involved. However, it wasn't until the late 20th century that a fuller understanding was achieved, finally identifying the fundamental mechanism which drives the entire living world. This is not widely understood even today.

This takes us back to the cell, or more precisely the external cell wall. Life in all its immense variety is driven in the end by a naturally occurring electrochemical reaction. The mechanism involves the spontaneous flow of positively and negatively charged ions across the cell wall, back and forth continuously, using gates or channels, some designed to let only ions of one particular element pass, say potassium or sodium ions. The in and out movements of some of the ions in effect react against each other, some being positively charged, others negatively, creating a continuously calibrated in-out rhythm many times per second. In this way the movement of ions creates an electric potential between the inside and outside of the cell, in an exquisite rhythmic dance.

A key end product of all this is our friend adenosine triphosphate, the all-purpose energy fuel of living things. It is this fuel which drives all signalling within living things, enabling heartbeat, breathing, digestion, muscular movement, indeed all brain activities, including thinking and consciousness. In short, this beautifully sensitive dance around the walls of every cell sums up what life is and how it differs from the non-living world.

And yet even this is only part of the picture. All the processes outlined here are in fact guided at the molecular level by information in the body's own DNA. Life in the end is a self-reproducing system. In order to make life, it appears, first of all you have to have – life!

Discovering this whole process was surely one of the epic events of 20th century biology, comparable to the discovery of the double helical structure of DNA. But how exactly does electric power drive the living world? How does this work in detail? A whole new field of bioelectricity, addressing these questions, has in recent years begun to open up. We can look forward to exciting new discoveries in the next decade or two.

Hard on the heels of this, one further new field of investigation may be about to open up. All the remarkable workings of living tissue may perhaps rest ultimately on an atomic and molecular dimension, and beyond this on the bizarre logic of the quantum world within the atom. In what ways might these two worlds of quantum physics and molecular biology interconnect? Work on a new field, quantum biology, is only just getting underway. Prospects look exciting.

Taking a wider view, it now does appear that the living world is in some sense at home in this universe after all. It's not just that living things are made from the commonest of materials, hydrogen, water and carbon compounds. All this is 'brought to life', as we say, all this incredible working complexity is driven, deep down, by forces in some degree akin to those which hold the atom together and drive the very fabric of a material universe. So it turns out that perhaps life is not a freak, not an alien intruder in a dead universe. On the contrary it does seem fairer to say that life is a natural consequence of the very fabric of this material, chemical, electromagnetic, space-time creation.

One further point concerns the scale of this universe, which was the subject of Chapter 1 of this book. It is all very human to think that because the universe is so huge, we ourselves must necessarily be vanishingly insignificant – the one idea seems to follow logically from the other. But consider the endless mass of intricate detail which goes to make up a living creature – even a field mouse, say, or the little Arabidopsis plant, let alone a thinking human being. The detailed miracle of these creatures, products of the evolution of life on earth, cannot help but excite our admiration. If we are indeed tiny and insignificant, we are also wonders of a staggeringly intricate process, and our very smallness is perhaps part of that wonder. You might say we are like living jewels, only infinitely more intricate.

Chapter 8

Once upon a time – how life came to be

The glory of life today

The natural world can speak to us in a powerful, wordless language, reaching under the surface of our conscious attention. Something deep in us responds to the visual symmetry of a spider's web. The elegant patterns of the sunflower seed head seem to reflect the rhythm of how it grew in time. We marvel at the teeming world in every cubic centimetre of pond water and equally at the army of underground fungi which help plants to take up water and nutrients.

But perhaps it's the sheer variety of nature's creatures which catches our admiration most of all – the cassowary with its exotic headgear, the sifaka lemur, the tree pangolin, the cougar, the honey possum, the snowdrop, the yucca plant and the baobab tree, the skink, the coelacanth, the mudskipper and the sea squirt, the deep sea anglerfish, the pond-skater, the Camberwell beauty and the bedbug, the orang-utan and the nine-banded armadillo, each authentically and triumphantly itself.

The great sweep of the history of life reveals pattern and unity in this diversity. Pick up a piece of chalk and you hold the exoskeletal remains of tiny marine creatures who lived and died in immense numbers some ninety million years before there were humans to wonder at them. A lump of coal is mute witness to the very first forests to spread unchallenged over the earth's land masses 350 million years ago.

We know from an abundant fossil record that South America, Africa, India, Madagascar, Australia and Antarctica once formed a single great continent (known today as Gondwanaland). When this broke up, Antarctica drifted south towards the pole while life on the new island masses of Australia and Madagascar diversified in different directions, suddenly both isolated and liberated from further continental competition, creating a world of lemurs on Madagascar and of marsupials on Australia. Meanwhile Africa and India drifted north, eventually colliding with a Eurasian land mass, throwing up the Himalayas and the whole ripple of high mountain ranges extending from Indonesia to Europe. The Mediterranean Sea and the three thousand seven hundred mile Great African Rift Valley formed partly from this slow-moving crash, which also pushed above water level the chalk, limestone and coal-bearing landscapes of Britain. (This collision continues today at a steady pace of a few centimetres per year, that is a few metres per century or a few tens of kilometres every million years.)

At various locations across the world, perhaps most famously the Burgess Shale in the Canadian Rocky Mountains, are remains of some of the earliest multi-celled creatures on earth, dating from some 550 million years back. The design features of some of these species, especially the ones which in the end did not survive to modern times, seem to our eyes so exotic as to be unreal. One of the most celebrated is opabinia, once upon a time a small marine creature a few centimetres long. Opabinia was graced by five eyes on stalks and a trunk about a third of its entire body length, ending in a claw-like structure, and it steered itself by means of a fan-shaped tail. (I assure you I'm not making this up. Do look it up online.) Another small creature was aptly named hallucigenia. Recently experts suddenly realised that they had been interpreting its remains upside-down, mistaking its head for its rear end!

There is a sublime creative power in nature, an exuberant ingenuity capable of inventing new worlds apparently from nothing. It works with vast oceans of time as its raw material. In time it brought us to being, as if from nowhere.

While it 'only' took somewhere over half a billion years for the whole panoply of multi-celled life to spread through the oceans, invade the land masses and populate the skies, it took a preceding few billions of years to create the foundations of all this, especially the foundation of all animals and plants, the eukaryotic cell. But going further back, before even this remarkable development had got started, it took a further several hundred million years for the ultimate wonder, the emergence of a living world by natural processes from non-living matter. We need to keep these two quite different stages separate in our minds, so we will consider them in turn, first the three billion years or so which it took to make the foundations of life as we know it today, and then the hundreds of millions of years before that, during which the very first prototypes of life emerged on this planet.

The striking thing is that all this most likely began with a mass of interacting biochemical molecules, and the whole development took advantage of only random error rate and natural processes of selection. In the light of this, the dazzling complexity of life today is surely living witness to an exceedingly ancient heritage.

Ancient foundations

Although the billions of years before multi-celled life can sometimes seem to us to be inordinately, perhaps tediously long, they did achieve a number of exceedingly complex developments which were crucial to the formation of our own world. Bacteria and viruses emerged, which today colonise our bodies and the mitochondria and chloroplasts which live and work inside living cells. Solar power, photosynthesis, was harnessed, the basis of the food energy of all life today. Living cells emerged, the building blocks of all plants and animals, with their spectacular complexity, in both prokaryotic and eukaryotic models. Perhaps above all, a by-product of this early world of single-celled creatures began to accumulate, first in the oceans of planet earth and then also in its atmosphere – oxygen.

It would be a mistake, however, to assume that multi-celled life was the main result of this three billion year interlude, and that single-celled creatures subsequently fell into decline. It is now understood, in fact, that there are more bacteria guesting in a human body than there are the body's own cells. We, then, like all plants and animals alive today, are made up of a host structure, i.e. our body with its trillions of cells, plus countless guests. The bacteria which live inside us have their own DNA, they are not directly related to us, they just colonise us, from head to toe, from skin to digestive system, in endless varieties. Single-celled life, it has been calculated, in fact makes up well over half of the total biomass of life on earth today. You could say that multi-celled creatures, when they finally arrived, represented a major opportunity for single-celled creatures to expand, providing a whole new habitat to exploit. Just as mitochondria had earlier colonised the interior of each body cell, so countless different species of bacteria then colonised the body between and around the cells, many of them proving to be very useful in maintaining the body's health and welfare.

Recent work has revealed a complex continuous interaction between the body's cell DNA and its population of bacteria. The body is evidently a proactive manager, protecting some species of bacteria, attacking others, and diverting yet others to more useful work.

But bacteria are not the only colonists inhabiting multi-celled bodies. We all know about viruses, from HIV to Ebola and the many different strains of the common flu bug, but these are viruses which invade us from outside. We may be less aware that there are also millions of different virus species living permanently in the bodies of every multi-celled species, just like bacteria do. Viruses are neither multi-celled nor even single-celled entities, but are simply relatively short strands of DNA or RNA packaged in some kind of protective membrane, no doubt survivors of an ancient era. Crucially, today they can only reproduce inside another living form. Not all viruses cause disease, many are helpful, some in fact protect us from other more menacing viruses!

Someone has compared the body to a tropical rainforest or a coral reef as an example of prolific, teeming ecological diversity. It is even claimed that animals, not least humans, might not have evolved so successfully without the many-sided assistance of both bacteria and viruses.

Perhaps the most momentous development during this entire three billion years before multi-celled life emerged on earth was the achievement of molecular solar power, photosynthesis, a complex biochemical process in which sunlight, an apparently massless thing, generates a whole chain of chemical reactions which create sugars, a flexible fuel source for the many complex needs of living things. The process of photosynthesis is a long interconnection of different stages, in a way like the process of distillation, and this raises a question. How could this contorted process have ever come about by chance? Part of the answer may be that the whole process originally evolved as at least two, maybe more than two separate processes, each having previously evolved to achieve quite different purposes, then much later coming together.

It appears that this kind of thing is not uncommon within the evolution of life. Bird feathers, for example, may have evolved originally as insulation for dinosaur-like species, then proved useful as the first proto-birds started to glide among tree branches, perhaps flying for short stretches to evade capture. In the case of photosynthesis, once the total, joined-up process had successfully started working, its future would no doubt have been assured.

There may well have been all kinds of partial successes, halfway solutions and false starts along the way. Even more remarkable, this whole process was achieved by single-celled organisms some of which later invaded the cells of the earliest plants. Every plant cell today contains thousands of them, called chloroplasts, similar in some ways to mitochondria. Chloroplasts, in effect photosynthesis machines, are today the basis of the entire food chain of multi-celled life on earth.

Earliest prototypes of life?

But even remarkable achievements like photosynthesis, bacteria and the complex, advanced cells of later times are perhaps eclipsed by the original creation of living organisms from non-living molecules, quite possibly as far back as four billion years ago. How are we to begin to imagine this epic event taking place in an era so far removed from us?

It may have happened in stages. Long before the very earliest prototypes of living things eventually emerged, the likely biochemical ingredients were no doubt already there in abundance, scattered throughout deep space. These sophisticated organic molecules, natural products of the commonest elements in existence, would no doubt be already interacting spontaneously in a maze of complex varieties. Some might tend to have a catalytic effect on others, speeding up their creation, or inhibiting it, or switching between the two effects following some biochemical cue. At times catalytic chains may have developed, where A accelerates B, which in turn accelerates C, which accelerates D which accelerates A again. Our understanding of all this is still at an early stage, but a more detailed picture is steadily coming together.

Sooner or later these molecules could presumably have generated a whole series of joint ventures. Examples of long-term collaboration which proved to enhance chances of survival would therefore eventually become more widespread. As soon as a collaborative venture had become established, the need for some degree of protection from a chaotic outside world would become more and more urgent. Protective walls of varying effectiveness would have been tried, keeping out unwanted interference but allowing the entry of energy sources and expelling waste. This traffic in and out of the prototype cell wall then in time began to exploit naturally occurring molecular electric currents. In time these currents would become more efficient at sustaining a regular rhythm, creating a more or less inexhaustible supply of self-generated energy, potentially fuelling a whole range of biochemical processes.

The effectiveness of this may have improved only slowly over quite a period of time, but at some juncture came a take-off point, when a biochemical network became reliably self-sustaining, or as we would say today – alive! The run-up to life, then, may have come in a series of steps, each occurring spontaneously – catalytic chains, collaborative communities, external cell membranes and electricity flowing across them, the tapping of usable energy sources, like sunlight, and occurring alongside all this, the universal winnowing process of natural selection.

The cell probably achieved a degree of complexity right from early stages, and with the passage of time its sophistication would soon multiply exponentially. Over the three billion year span many different models of cell-building may have been attempted. Two forms survived, first the prokaryotic cell, of which bacteria are a good example, and maybe some time later the more elaborate eukaryotic cell, the foundation of all multi-celled life.

The sheer complexity of these cells goes some way to account for the enormous span of time it took to produce them. The immense complexity of the molecules, the experiments at various forms of organisation, the coming together of more and more complex collaborative arrangements, the growing efficiency of electric generation across cell walls, all this adds up to an immense story, and the end products were indeed remarkable. Someone using military comparisons has compared today's prokaryotic cell to a fighter plane, with its sophisticated control systems and its miles of wiring. The later eukaryotic model? This has been compared in its complexity to an aircraft carrier! Others, as we have seen, have compared it to a highly organised city state – all of this, remember, at the invisibly small scale of clusters of atoms and molecules. The human mind hesitates to believe that anything as hugely impressive as this could ever have come about by a process of selective culling and survival.

Some people have suggested that for the development of such a colossal degree of complexity even a span of three billion years may simply not have been enough. It is still possible that there may be further elaborations of Darwin's vision to be uncovered. In recent decades game theory has thrown light on the processes of extinction and survival. Quite soon the manifold roles of bacteria and viruses within every multi-celled life form may be better understood. Bacteria and other microorganisms appear to reproduce and evolve very much faster than most animals and plants. It is known that they also exchange bio-materials amongst themselves much more freely than their hosts, and this includes bacterial DNA. It appears possible that viruses in particular are occasionally successful at actually invading the host eukaryotic cell's nucleus, opening the possibility of altering parts of the DNA itself. Could something like this have acted as a catalyst, accelerating the whole evolutionary process?

The logic of this could take us further still. Perhaps our internal army of bacteria and viruses could have assisted not just the speed but the direction of evolutionary change. It is widely assumed that they acted sometimes not just as catalysts speeding up change, but as filters, attacking certain kinds of evolutionary experiments which didn't suit them, while favouring others. Could our bacterial and viral body guests have helped shape the process of all plant and animal evolution? At the moment we don't know this for certain, but perhaps we need to keep an open mind, scanning for new possibilities.

Another factor has been suggested. Perhaps some key stages

in the development of life had been already achieved before the earth actually formed. Amongst the deluge of ice and dust raining (or snowing) down on to the earth there may have been molecular combinations which could already be classified as self-replicating units, still perhaps dependent on an external energy source, or similar perhaps to viruses, not quite independently alive but on the way towards it.

When early life forms did arrive, on the other hand, they were probably not yet able to tap sunlight as an energy source. The impressive sophistication of photosynthesis suggests that it may have evolved sometime after the earliest life forms took shape. Presumably, then, there must have been living systems, including early forms of cells, thriving on the earth before the later, happy serendipity of photosynthesis. Early life, it seems, may not have depended on sunlight, although ours does.

When we consider the byzantine complexity of the living world, and then delve into the processes by which this complexity apparently arose, and then contemplate the oceans of time this evidently required, we may wish to pause for breath. This experience might be both humbling and exhilarating at one and the same time. Shall we take a few moments?

Chapter 9

The blind logic of time and change

Survival in Hades

No doubt it took a long span of time, perhaps half a billion years, before the first versions of life had become established on the young earth. But what then? What kind of conditions then helped life to survive and evolve for such an extraordinary stretch of time?

It seems likely that our galaxy could quickly annihilate all traces of life, but on the other hand it is actually remarkably empty of matter, and besides, our own little solar system appears to be perched out on one of our galaxy's spiral arms a very long way from the rather more crowded central hub. As we have seen, the inner core of the solar system, where the planets are, is something less than a light day across, whereas our nearest neighbour star of any size within the galaxy is more than four light years distant and the whole galaxy is some hundred thousand light years across. The volume of matter to empty space in our galaxy has been in fact compared to that of atomic particles inside an atom, which likewise appears to consist overwhelmingly of empty space.

Our solar system formed in a tiny corner of our galaxy some four and a half billion years ago out of a swirling mass of interstellar matter which came together by a naturally self-reinforcing spinning motion and the force of its own gravity, eventually forming a central ball and a number of planets, all spinning on their axes. The central ball gathered so much mass and gravitational pressure that it ignited.

Throughout the first billion years of this spiralling mass of rock and dust there were inevitably countless impacts of all sizes. This would make of the earth a seething, hot, volcanically active mass, truly a Hadean landscape. At sometime early in this period our earth, some experts believe, collided in a glancing blow with another planet of almost earth size in an impact of what must have been immense scale and violence. People have named this visitor Theia. It hit the earth with such force, people have concluded, that it knocked it away from its original angle of spin by more than 20 degrees – quite a smack, creating our seasonal climate variations. Some of the matter from Theia buried itself deep in the earth, quite possibly an impact whose force still echoes today in the tectonic movement of the continents across the surface of the earth. Other matter from both earth and Theia flew off into space, while some of it circled the earth, perhaps for a time like a ring of matter or perhaps a string of smaller satellites, eventually coalescing into the single ball of the moon.

This might explain the oddity that our moon represents in our solar system. Most moons are tiny, seen against their parent planet. Only our moon, and perhaps Pluto's largest moon, Charon, are of a mass in some degree comparable to their planet. It is thought that Charon might quite possibly have collided with Pluto in the same way that Theia collided with the earth.

There are probably other consequences of this impact. According to recent research, the earth's core is unusually warm for a planet of its size and distance from the sun. This heat apparently drives (or is driven by) the dynamic movement of molten iron in the earth's core. This in turn appears to generate the magnetic shield around our planet which protects life from damaging cosmic radiation. So the aptly named Hadean era of frequent impacts from surrounding space, although for a time it must have menaced the very existence of life, also seems to have created the rather special conditions for its longer-term survival.

Other major impacts presumably happened, perhaps not quite the size of Theia but involving massive rocks a good few scores of kilometres across. The first era of the earth's history no doubt saw further major impacts, unpredictable but still frequent. Mixed in with these, as we have seen, was a naturally occurring rain of smaller objects and particles, and perhaps these included volumes of ice falling over many millions of years, melting in a volcanically active earth and filling up the oceans which became characteristic of our planet. A few early forms of life on earth somehow survived these periodically threatening conditions. Life, then, despite the protecting magnetic shield and the abundant oceans, was no doubt severely tested and had to adapt and evolve just to survive during its first billion years on this earth. Maybe very little living tissue survived at the time, but what little did survive then proceeded to multiply more easily when times became calmer.

In time, as the solar system formed and more and more matter fell, there was simply less and less left to fall. The interplanetary spaces were increasingly cleared of debris. The sun itself, and perhaps also Jupiter and the other giant planets, in effect vacuumed up much of the remaining interplanetary matter, marshalling much of what was left into a ring of asteroids between the orbits of Mars and Jupiter, and a rather larger one beyond Neptune.

In the last half billion years, however, major impacts have still occurred, perhaps every few tens of millions of years, some causing major extinctions of living creatures. The volcanic activity within the earth, an equal source of menace to life on the planet, also took a long time to quieten down. The Great Permian Extinction, 251 million years ago, was probably caused by massive volcanic eruptions triggering abrupt climate cooling, wiping out the great majority of marine species as well as the first land forests.

Today's volcanic events, then, are faint echoes of a much more destructive past. Much smaller asteroids still streak across our skies every few decades – one was caught on camera above Chelyabinsk in Siberia in February 2013. NASA and other agencies are now working out ways of identifying asteroids which may be on a collision course with earth. (One sizable collision may happen, it is predicted, in the year 2136. Astronomers are already tracking the asteroid in question.) Nevertheless the pandemonium of the Hadean era did eventually subside, allowing the earth to become gradually calmer.

Oxygen accumulating

So it was in steadier but still uncertain conditions that a most radical development occurred, another twist in the game of survival in which a new form of life might eventually emerge. Oxygen seems to have been the key to this. For long a by-product of early single-celled life, it had been slowly accumulating in the oceans and later in the atmosphere, and although this substance was highly reactive and toxic, destructive in fact to many forms of life, for others much later in time it provided new opportunities. Exploiting these, a variety of new organisms began to develop more and more complex patterns of cooperation between individual cells. Life was once again responding to changing conditions by creating new opportunities to outrun them. Once again life no doubt went through the usual false starts before the first sustainable models of multi-celled life began to survive.

There are still surviving on the earth today one or two echoes of this time of experimenting with multi-celled cooperation. There is, for example, the strange case of the slime mould, which is normally content to exist as a colony of single-celled creatures, physically in touch but independent of each other. When danger threatens, however, or new food supplies are sensed, the colony moves off, travelling over the ground very much as if it were a single multi-celled creature. Then, when the emergency is over, the colony reverts to its single-celled state. Presumably other halfway experiments like this may once have existed, in some intermediate stage between single cells and closer associations, some eventually becoming permanent multi-celled creatures.

It is worth noting that today bacteria and other single-celled organisms often have elaborate chemical signalling systems which can enable them to coordinate defence or attack. The individual cells within a multi-celled organism also keep in regular chemical communication with each other, perhaps a more elaborate echo of the patterns in operation amongst bacteria. The origins of these inter-cell networks are no doubt very ancient.

All multi-celled life on the surface of the earth today is dependent on sunlight, which it exploits by means of photosynthesis. This process, involving the release of oxygen as a by-product, began perhaps two to three billion years back, when single-celled Cyanobacteria first tapped sunlight for energy.

This means that today's living world makes use of a substance, oxygen, which is largely the by-product of an earlier living world, a world of single-celled creatures far back in the past. So today's living world of multi-celled creatures lives off a key by-product of a previous living world.

This recalls the modern idea, sometimes referred to under the name of Gaia, which compares nature on this earth to a single organism, an organism which has adapted itself to the earth's environment, thus protecting itself more effectively. Perhaps, indeed, this is what you might expect of a system which has been subject to long eons of natural selection. Over time new forms of life have successfully embedded themselves into this new environment of sunlight, water and oxygen.

Swathes of culling, oceans of time

It does seem that for life to evolve successfully over time, it needs some favourable times mixed with times of really quite severe challenge. Perhaps this is one of the paradoxes of evolution. In the long-term life seems to thrive on a mix of the two, stability and challenge, but it seems to be the times of challenge which generate most of the truly radical evolutionary changes.

Our planet seems to have gone through a uniquely stimulating mix of climate stability and change, with typically a few score million years of relative stability alternating with short periods of volcanic disruption or asteroid impact, often killing off many hitherto prolific species. This is what has given to the earth its series of geological eras. What lies behind this apparent long-term rhythm of alternating stability and disruption? Some people have suggested that the disruptions may have been influenced by events originating beyond our solar system, or perhaps even beyond our galaxy.

Charles Darwin's startling vision was of an ever-present winnowing process in spontaneous operation throughout nature, quite often gentle but on occasion exceedingly swift and harsh. This is such a striking idea that to some people it may seem at first glance unlikely. It's not just that it accounts for the development of the vast range of living things over long eons of time by means of a single uniting principle. The more difficult thing to swallow is that all this happens as a result of spontaneous, accidental events. From sheer random complexity, pattern naturally emerges. Some patterns are favoured and survive to reproduce abundantly, others notably less so, while others again may soon die out without reproducing. This kind of essentially statistical difference, often apparently quite minor, can sometimes produce significant change in just a few generations.

Reactions to Darwin's idea were confused and took time to mature. At first it was so arrestingly simple and so surprising that for a time it was the butt of jokes. Some people rejected it because it appeared to do without a divine agent. Some thought it was about survival of the most ruthlessly aggressive, and this idea was unfortunately influential for a good few decades in political thinking. Some early opposition to it, indeed, came not just from the religious right but from the political left, since it appeared to leave no room for compassion and human solidarity, or indeed for hope. Yet today, a full century and a half later, Darwin's vision is understood somewhat differently.

In particular it took time to realise that in this universal process cooperation was perhaps at least as important as aggressive competition. Even at the very earliest stages of life on earth, living creatures often had a more assured survival rate if they cooperated with others. Forming alliances, exchanging mutual benefits, close symbiotic relationships, groups of species co-evolving together, this cooperation no doubt took many different forms. Viruses and bacteria, for example, were co-opted in vast number within the bodies of multi-celled creatures. Violent aggression, on the other hand, was frequently just too risky, and therefore may have remained relatively rare. In many cases, indeed, it may have been selected out – over time the most aggressive individuals simply wouldn't have survived.

But the striking thing is that sheer random chance had also played a key part in the whole process. Sometimes a species or a whole ecosystem successfully survived over a long period of time, but then was quickly swept away. In other eras natural selection appears to have been quiescent – random changes would continue to occur, but it would be hard to see any obvious natural advantage.

This is awesome to contemplate and it may take us time to get our head round it and get used to it, but oddly enough it is relatively simple to explain. It appears to be the nature of life to do this. Any absence of this ubiquitous mechanism of change would be harder to explain.

This universal mechanism of selection evidently works at many levels, at the level of the ecosystem and equally of individual creatures – and of the herds of bacteria and viruses colonising every corner of their bodies. It certainly operates at the level of the genome, expressed in DNA code in every cell. At that level, indeed, change can happen at a relatively fast pace, and an error rate therefore accumulates relatively frequently. Sometimes, for example, a sequence of DNA can be copied twice instead of just once, or it is moved to a different place, perhaps one with a similar starting signal but rather different consequences.

'Mistakes' like these are liable to occur every so often. Not surprisingly, many life forms have developed some form of internal policing system double-checking the copying process and correcting errors, but in some cases even this can be perhaps a bit rough and ready, and is never entirely foolproof. Nature, then, always exuberantly creative, always on the move, adapts existing forms, cobbles things together, but, perhaps surprisingly, never looks forward, never anticipates future possibilities. The whole process of natural selection is in this sense effectively blind.

Maybe the process of evolution has itself evolved over time. Today's world, after all, is the inheritor of billions of years of life on earth, and any new experiment has to compete with life forms already in place. Back in the earliest eras it may have been more like a free-for-all, in which error rates were sky high, complex molecules meeting up by chance, some by chance sticking together more easily than others. Many eons later, however, existing molecular communities would sooner or later get round to limiting the scale of error rates, evolving primitive correction routines. Once evolution had really got into motion, it would perhaps have been more advantageous to protect existing communities than to continue with the old free-for-all. The situation, in other words, was changing perfectly naturally. Evolution was itself evolving.

In all this drama one point perhaps stands out. The evolution of the living world, in all its spectacular grandeur, happened without either forethought or intention or forward planning

– these are by-products of advanced intelligence, itself a late outcome of the process of evolution. So the whole evolution of life evidently happened without understanding. Understanding came later.

Theme 4

Understanding understanding

Chapter 10

Echoes from the dream time

The awakening of the past

In the later decades of the 19th century reports began to appear describing discoveries of human-like skulls and other remains in Africa and elsewhere, but for a long time few people saw the significance of this. Later, the understanding of early human archaeology began to take shape, and its implications were startling. Here were the beginnings of a whole new subject of study, human prehistory, connecting two subjects which had hitherto been thought of as entirely separate, history and biology.

Once the early Egyptians, at 3000 BCE, were seen as the very dawn of human history. Today the origins of the Neolithic Revolution, the earliest spread of agriculture and permanent settlements, is now being dated at anything between 8 and 12 thousand years ago. Cave paintings discovered in France and Spain are now dated at 17–22 thousand years ago, and some in Spain as old as 30 thousand years ago, and other artefacts found in central Europe and Russia date to an apparent cultural flourishing around 30–35 thousand years ago and even further back. Now it is widely agreed that ancestors of ours, Homo sapiens, spread out beyond their historic home in Africa and began an epic migration around the coasts of Asia some 60–70 thousand years ago. Some people have pushed this event back well before 100 thousand years ago. Presumably humans had been evolving in Africa over many tens of millennia before that.

This may mean that we are all Africans in origin. Within the ample framework of geological time, moreover, all this happened really quite recently, so it appears that in evolutionary terms we, the entire human race, are in fact all close cousins.

There is even a suggestion from modern genomics that at one point adverse conditions maybe 70–80 thousand years back had reduced the entire population of Homo sapiens to a few tens of thousands. If this is so, then we are all descended from a common, really quite recent stock.

Going further back, archaeological evidence points to the existence in Europe and Asia of human people (although not Homo sapiens) going back 500–700 thousand years ago, and at Atapuerca in northern Spain this date has been pushed back to as much as 1.2 million years ago. It looks likely that these people originally migrated out of Africa at a much earlier date. So-called Homo Neanderthalensis lived in Europe and the Near East from some 300 thousand years ago, dying out apparently as late as 40 thousand years ago, that is, probably coexisting alongside modern humans for a good few thousand years. Another subspecies, so-called Denisovans, lived in Asia at about the same time, and recent discoveries in South Africa have uncovered remains of another human group, so-called Homo Naledi, living about 300,000 years ago. Finally, on the island of Flores in Southeast Asia excavations have identified an apparently diminutive subspecies, suitably named Homo Floresiensis. This early human group died out apparently as recently as 15 thousand years ago.

Going back much farther again, Homo erectus, our earliest recognisably human ancestor, lived in Africa and parts of Asia from as early as 2 million years ago, until as recently as 70 thousand years ago. This means that Homo erectus evidently survived for very much longer on this earth than we modern humans have up to now, and this may be equally true of Homo Neanderthalensis. These were truly human people, not intelligent apes; they were very like us indeed, very much closer to us than to any of our closest related species alive today.

Still further back, remains of creatures we could call semi-human, classified by the name Australopithecus, have been found in various locations across Africa, dating from between 2 and 4 million years ago. Australopithecus had many features similar to later humans and to other primate species. Some argue that the growth of the modern human brain may have been favoured by a diet rich in fish during that era, as the skills of diving and trapping were mastered. Still farther back, the common genetic link between modern humans and our closest living cousins, chimpanzees, bonobos and gorillas, is now estimated at some 7–10 million years ago. And in the few million years before that, going back as far as 12–14 million years ago, was an era in which still more evolutionary developments seem to have originated. This is sometimes referred to as the era of the planet of the apes, an era when many species of intelligent apes were flourishing and various key human features were already emerging – larger brains, upright stature, dexterous hands and an extended childhood.

So our human species, Homo sapiens, although certainly remarkable, has evidently evolved by stages from non-human predecessors over several million years. Even more strikingly, different species of humans appear to have coexisted over the same territory in the same time span. The stages by which our ancestors made the remarkable leap into modern humanity are now established and are becoming better understood.

Were these other human species truly our ancestors? Did they interbreed with the first modern humans? Recently the field of genomics has come up with intriguing evidence. There does seem to be a degree of similarity between the DNA of modern humans and both Neanderthals and Denisovans, and this does suggest a limited degree of interbreeding. At the same time it seems likely that modern Homo sapiens simply outcompeted the others. They hunted more lethally and were probably altogether more flexible in adapting to changing conditions as Ice Ages advanced and retreated. (Some believe Homo sapiens became dominant especially when we began to hunt with dogs, although others think this came much later.)

Perhaps to our surprise, we can now legitimately view the Neanderthals, Denisovans, Homo Naledi, the Flores people, and even the earlier Homo erectus, as our long-lost relatives. We modern humans, then, are no longer like solitary cuckoos in the nest. We have acquired a past and with it a host of ancestor cousins, almost like discovering a whole new stepfamily. We are no longer orphans.

And our evolution continues. It now seems likely that we have inherited a complex of behaviour which is remarkably open-ended – now we just need to understand it better. In short, we need to understand understanding itself. But maybe we will eventually prove to be quite good at this. Maybe this sophisticated understanding has been 'selected in', the ultimate proof being that we are still here, asking these questions. So if we listen to the echoes from our dream time, the many long millennia of our distant past, we may be able to hear more than just one voice, more than just sounds of aggression and violence. The key to our future, our continuing evolution, may turn out to be a sophisticated capacity to understand ourselves and our surroundings. Perhaps in the end this is what may transform our future, and in the process, transform us. Understanding will be key.

Two thousand millennia

What were conditions like for our early human forebears during the many long millennia preceding modern historical times, the millennia in which so many of our instincts were presumably laid down? While our earliest predecessor meriting the name of human, Homo erectus, may have appeared as long as two million years ago, the first truly modern humans, Homo sapiens, seem to date from some two or three hundred thousand years ago. Let's keep these two dates clear. Some of our most important traits may have been laid down during the 2–3 hundred millennia of

Homo sapiens, the later of the two periods, while others may have been inherited from a good deal farther back, from the days of our probable ancestor, Homo erectus.

Questions arise. What developments took place during the period between 2 million years ago and 200 thousand years ago? In what ways did things change during the period between 200 thousand and, say, 50 thousand years ago, just before the era of the so-called cultural flowering in Europe, and between then and ten thousand years ago, when agriculture and the modern era of human history finally got underway?

What was life like during these long stretches of time? It's hard to imagine such a very different environment when we know so very little with any degree of certainty, but nevertheless we can sketch in outline some likely features of very early human life. A nomadic hunter-gatherer lifestyle, for example, no doubt could only support an exceedingly low density of population. One writer has said, perhaps with just a bit of exaggeration, that the entire population of the northern half of Britain at that time would have barely filled a double-decker bus! Even the earliest farmers migrating from the eastern Mediterranean only a few thousand years ago (like the earliest builders of Stonehenge or the inhabitants of Skara Brae in the Orkney Islands) were pretty thin on the ground by later standards, but the hunters who had lived during the many long preceding millennia before them were a good deal more sparsely scattered even than that.

In these circumstances a steady level of violence between individuals and small groups may have been a routine part of daily life but larger-scale battles between clans and alliances were perhaps more rare. True warfare and conquest was probably the product of a very much later time, associated with the rise of early agriculture, when the first sizable permanent settlements were established and the earliest mini-empires arose, and with that a much more sustained population rise and a consequent struggle for key resources. The large-scale slaughter of true warfare, then, may have been a consequence of humanity's much more recent success in peopling the earth in more substantial numbers.

During the long formative era before all this, with tiny nomadic populations and vast stretches of virgin land, cautious avoidance and maybe further migration would surely have been on many occasions a wiser counsel than hot-blooded aggression. For early humans, as indeed for many other species throughout the animal world, the consequences of aggression were often mortally risky and had to be weighed with care. Much of the time it would have made more sense to see other bands of humans as potential allies in battling against the persistent menace of non-human predators in the surrounding forest or grassland.

Some have speculated that human intelligence in the very early pre-sapiens times had specialised in certain immediately practical tasks. For example, evolutionary pressure may have favoured the development of a detailed geographical knowledge of surrounding territory. It would have paid handsomely to remember where predators habitually lurked or patrolled, where smaller prey could reliably be found – fish, fowl, rodents, for example – or plants which were good to eat or good for healing – or for poisoning. Another kind of practical intelligence might have been technical, including the making of an ever-increasing range of tools – whole books have been written about the development of the early hand-axe with its elegantly-shaped flint striking edge. Planning more complex, more shrewdly executed hunting campaigns would require advanced social intelligence, strengthening bonds between individuals in family and clan.

Later, building on this essentially practical base, a more flexible, more speculative intelligence could then have emerged, alongside the earliest forerunners of language. In time came a more highly developed skill in imagining future situations, an enhanced ability to plan, to foresee other worlds and other possibilities. Alongside this came a growing capacity to understand other minds, to see and predict the intentions of others, and an early awareness that good and bad could apply to everyone in the group alike. Here were early hints of a later instinct for rudimentary law and morality, crucial in moderating hot-headed aggression.

Finally, after a long passage of time the key factors in our humanity might have begun to come together with the emergence of symbolic narratives and ritual ceremonies, bonding mechanisms familiar to us today, creating a cultural capital which could be passed down the generations, in short, the beginnings of a folk memory.

The development of early language would have gone hand in hand with these other innovations. Human language and human reason, then, probably evolved together from deeper, more urgently practical needs.

The lens of language

It is so easy to take it for granted, but human language is remarkable. Just to begin with, for language to develop there had to be a whole series of physical developments, of the larynx, tongue, palate and entire mouth apparatus. These are in themselves very complex, so they are unlikely to have happened in just a few centuries. It evidently required ample stretches of time, perhaps many tens of millennia. The ear too had to develop an incredible degree of sensitivity, an ability to pick up fine differences in the sounds we produced, for example the difference between p and b, t and d, f and v, ah and eh, ih and ee. We do take this for granted, but the fine distinctions involved are truly minute.

Alongside all this there had to be accompanying developments in the brain, enabling us to grasp the logic of grammar and syntax, by any standards an even more impressive achievement.

Human languages by their nature impose on the external world a framework of grammatical understanding, dividing it up into things, events, qualities and relationships (that is, broadly, nouns, verbs, adjectives/adverbs, and prepositions/conjunctions). Humans, then, understand their world in terms of things which have qualities attached to them and which interact with each other in essentially straightforward ways.

So we humans need to make sense of our world and to communicate this to each other, using essentially simple terms. In time this led to a whole human world of cause and effect within a framework of space and time. In very much later times this then laid down the foundation for a scientific investigation of our world.

Many species are in some degree social, often operating on some kind of extended family grouping. Usually there is an upper limit to this group size, often correlating with the natural limits of food sources. Crucially, though, each individual has to spend time bonding with others in the group, creating a vital web of loyalty, often carried out by mutual grooming. This is slow, time-consuming work, and this too limits group size.

Modern humans are spectacularly a social species with a sophisticated brain, enabling each individual to bond with a much larger home group, and the acquisition of language has enabled bonding by conversational interaction, greatly expanding the physical limits of bonding rituals. It has been estimated that each human being today can easily recognise up to 150 acquaintances or friends, and the development of hierarchies has hugely multiplied the number of others with whom we can bond in some sense. Language also creates narratives, stories telling of other people in other situations and facing other dilemmas. To this day humans are addicted to stories of all kinds.

But beyond this our evolution has given us a really quite impressive array of other bonding mechanisms. Just think, for example, of the power of music to move people and bring them together in large numbers across today's world. It has been suggested that music and language had common origins – early ritual incantations and poems were quite possibly sung rather than spoken. Add to this the whole variety of games, dances, rituals and play routines. Humans have a strong liking for games and events which involve agreed rules.

Equally fundamental is laughter, a quintessentially human inheritance, allowing people to relax together and extend a degree of trust to each other, an ancient and potent creator of bonding. Finally just consider the power of tears, a behaviour originally rooted in the need to keep the eyes protected and lubricated, then adapted to transmit all kinds of social messages, powerfully bonding people together. Consider how a good story, or even music on its own, can bring a lump to the throat and stimulate the tear ducts! Consider how powerfully tears can stimulate sympathy and create solidarity, even between strangers.

Traits and skills like these enable us to bond with each other in numbers well beyond the limits of extended family and immediate clan. Arguably, in fact, they can enable us to empathise with any of our fellow humans anywhere on earth. Consider our responses to TV reports of natural disasters, even on the other side of the world.

But there is a lot more to human intelligence than bonding mechanisms and the hunger to understand. The human mind can be above all both creative and contrary. Humans do have a capacity for great cruelty, yet this strangely exists alongside a persistent sensitivity to morality. Humour, perhaps the most endearingly contrary of human traits, can playfully subvert certainties, a power which may be in reality essential for our sanity or even our survival in intolerable situations. Humour is often underrated, but it does make people laugh together and relax together. But amid all this, perhaps the most sublime and most inspiring of all human capacities, mysteriously allied to our pervasive hunger to understand, is the equally pervasive magic spell of beauty.

In the end it is the breadth and subtlety of human intelligence and its anarchic creativity which may reassure us in dangerous times. Above all it can be highly adaptive in unpredictable situations.

All this is perhaps of particular interest for us today, when our own greed, aggression and fear, still defining much of the political agenda, threaten to seriously damage our world. Some people respond to this with deep pessimism, assuming that greed and aggression are unchangeable instincts and concluding that we are all doomed. War, it is often assumed, is simply built into our genes. This pessimistic view rests on an assumption that our prehistory was rough and ruthless, but perhaps it is this modern era, the last ten thousand years, which has been rough and ruthless, with its politics of conquest and its capacity for murderous large-scale violence.

Warlike behaviour, then, may just possibly be an essentially modern symptom, a feature most characteristic of the last ten thousand years. This human capacity for inflicting slaughter has been compared, in fact, to the dysfunctional behaviour observed in other species, notably in rats, in conditions of abnormal overcrowding or high stress. Perhaps the uncontrolled aggression of modern times is dysfunctional in that sense, a response to overcrowding and perhaps the stress of continuous, rapid change. This is hardly a reason for optimism, but maybe Homo sapiens has also acquired other counterbalancing instincts long before all this, acquired during the long millennia of our prehistory.

Of course it is hazardous to predict the future in today's chaotically complex world, but perhaps we need to be wary of simple-minded doomsayers. Crucially, many of our human traits were laid down in a time when our numbers were tiny, and when our daily environment in forest or grassland was a dangerous place to be. Today we find ourselves in a very different place but still a dangerous place to be.

Faced with real danger, our inherited instincts need not always lead us to risky aggression, but can also produce caution, alertness, dialogue, bonding and a far-sighted anticipation of danger. But perhaps above all, in our early history it was a hunger to understand that was often the key to our survival. Perhaps it still is.

Survival and aggression

It was Tennyson who gave the Victorian world the phrase 'Nature, red in tooth and claw'. In time this combined with Darwin's idea of the survival of the fittest, and this in time somehow produced the idea of the survival of the most aggressive. This idea seems to have caught the public imagination – aggression, after all, had been with us, we thought, from early times, and wars, we assumed, had been a consistent feature of human history. The continually evolving technology of war then produced the truly horrific slaughter of the first modern, truly industrialised war, the American Civil War, breaking out very shortly after Darwin's great book was published. Half a century later this was followed by the contagious madness of the early 20th century world wars, leading to an abyss of truly unspeakable events, events which still stun the human imagination.

The idea that humans have survived in part thanks to this kind of aggression is still widely accepted, but maybe it's time we gave this some sharper, more sceptical attention. A modern war can destroy everything, wiping out whole civilisations, perhaps even blocking the possibility of long-term recovery, like a gigantic volcanic event. Perhaps the risks of this kind of insane logic will quite soon have become too much of a menace to everyone's long-term survival to be a realistic policy option. At least let us hope that our leaders will eventually have the good sense to see this. But sadly it may yet take a few more hugely destructive exchanges first, possibly even nuclear exchanges, before we finally catch on.

Where did this propensity for high risk slaughter begin? How far back in these long millennia of human origins did this find its earliest expression? Right from earliest times, indeed right from prehuman times, an inborn aggressive instinct had to be finely balanced by a capacity to find less hazardous ways around danger. This is true for many species. Overconfidence or impatience could often lead to dire consequences, especially for a small group. It would have been seen as seriously bad news, a kind of elementary stupidity which needed to be punished, weeded out quickly before it threatened the group's very survival. Some writers have even suggested that impulsive hotheads could have been exiled or even executed for putting the group into mortal danger.

In many species back then, aggression would be often about semi-ritualised displays of challenge, mock battle and submission, all designed to avoid unnecessary harm or bloodshed. (In our own species we can maybe recognise the roots of modern sporting rivalry.) From the very earliest times, then, peace-making skills had to be cultivated alongside the skills of violent conflict.

Perhaps in a strange way nothing much has changed since then. The old skills of long-term peace-building and risk-avoidance, honed during the many millennia of our prehistory, have perhaps come back centre stage in modern times. Our immediate environment has become mortally risky to us once again, only this time we are, as the saying goes, our own worst enemy.

Yet the early remains of Homo sapiens speak eloquently, with a delicate skull and slender bones, sometimes referred to as feminized features. Here was no reliance on muscle power or specialised diets. These modern humans were generalists and long-distance runners – not as fast as many other creatures, just persistent. It is claimed they could outrun almost any prey. They could certainly out-think any prey. This new capacity to understand, to see round a situation, might fit them for almost any season or any danger – perhaps a case of survival of the wisest, the farthest-seeing?

At some point in the region of forty thousand years ago the original primeval conditions were changing. By this time Homo sapiens had expanded out of its homeland in Africa, around the coasts of south and east Asia and into the Eurasian land mass. The fossil record suggests that by this time our ancestors may have been hunting several large species to extinction. By this time we had also outcompeted our cousin Homo Neanderthalensis. A growing stream of newly-acquired skills would have extended our horizons. The new art of cooking would have greatly improved our diet, and the skills of sewing would have enabled us to cope with a changing climate in altogether new ways. It was this balance of skills, not just war skills, which were naturally selected, ensuring our survival in a dangerous world.

Soon there would be time for other new concerns, rock paintings, bodily decoration, sympathetic magic, herbal healing remedies, musical skills, more elaborate ceremonies. Humans had started to bond not just with each other but with the land which they increasingly saw as theirs, as part of who they were. This land was still alive with unknown menace but also full of magic and beauty. The forests and the lakes were the home of good as well as evil spirits. The first stirrings of art and religion were becoming evident.

At this very, very early stage in our prehistory the stars were still incomprehensible, organized agriculture a dream still far in the future, large-scale warfare perhaps simply unimaginable. But with the new tool of language, a slow but irreversible rise in understanding was at last underway.

Chapter 11

From biochemistry to experience

Common wizardry

How is it possible to sum up the human brain in human words? How can we account for the workings of consciousness and the mind? Words can describe this at a certain perhaps simple level, but I doubt if they can do it in all its splendour anything like full justice.

All the workings of the mind rest on neural systems of truly unimaginable complexity, and in some ways this matches the awesome complexities of the natural world. Previous chapters have explored the endless intricacy of the biochemistry of life and of the evolutionary processes whereby it was brought to its present state of being. But even in a universe characterised by wonders like these, the human brain does seem to stand out in its own highly unique way.

It's not the zillions of neurons that make it so distinctive, but the way these neurons organise themselves – yes organise themselves – and perhaps above all it's what they finally achieve. Stated in purely numerical terms, the human brain has tens of billions of individual neurons, and each neuron is in contact with thousands of others. So in this super-connected internal world no neuron ever acts alone. Each one influences and is influenced by countless others, which influence myriads of others again, making a difference to things only when acting in concert with whole networks of others. So the brain sees only what it is primed to see, what it expects to see, and filters out most of the rest.

But it's the outcome of all this which commands our special attention. The purpose of all this networking of countless neurons is to create nothing less than an inner universe, held and continuously updated in a kind of brain coding which is ultimately biochemical. It achieves this, moreover, at an unimaginable level of networks within networks within networks within networks. Conscious awareness, moreover, is only a small part of this internal workshop. Neurosurgeons describe the intimate delicacy of brain tissue – touch a particular point and a bizarre mix of memories and dreams flood into consciousness, touch it too roughly and lasting damage, paralysis or even death can ensue.

Any perfectly humdrum activity will typically involve up to thirty centres in different brain locations in instant, flickering, evanescent dialogue, somehow, somewhere coordinated and selectively remembered from one moment to another. Delicate, vulnerable and in its own way immensely powerful, if ever there was a magical world, out-soaring even the breathtaking wonders of the surrounding creation, it is right here, inside us.

Consider the perfectly normal workings of memory. Imagine for example that you are rereading a novel after a gap of twenty years or so. Some details have been accurately remembered, and signals of recognition come to us readily enough. Other details are curiously compressed, and still others appear to have been forgotten entirely. As we keep reading, it can feel for a while as if this is a first time. Yet once memory has been refreshed, further details re-emerge, as though from the dead. Typically this is accompanied by an unmistakable experience of recognising something we thought we had irretrievably lost. An evidently sophisticated editing and storage process has been busy, and we haven't even been consulted.

Consider the majestic faculty of human reason, in origin perhaps the inheritor of a number of more limited prehuman forerunners. Apparently it is designed to pick out pattern and simplicity against a background of immense complexity, employing its twin tools, words and numbers. It does all this in aid of a driving inborn need to make some kind of sense of our surroundings, partly because this can underpin a yearning need for security.

Then consider consciousness, for some time in recent years the focus of intense interdisciplinary investigation and pondering, still a fascinating and enduring puzzle. Alongside memory and reason the human brain apparently edits and presents this strange, private, continuous film-like script, set into the present moment from a cacophony of inputs, prioritising and integrating them on behalf of an apparently single centre of operations. You might say that the brain generates consciousness and consciousness awakens the mind. Perhaps above all, the mind injects urgency, vividness and drama and makes things memorable. Consciousness, then, presents as narrative drama the very stuff of our lives, desire and fear, curiosity and caution, adventure and security, all finely interwoven. The fact is, however, that consciousness is part of something more remarkable even than all that. Consciousness is part of the extraordinary feat – it is tempting to call it magical – in which biochemistry becomes experience.

All this is certainly remarkable. The brain records and continuously updates our experience of life, day by day and second by second. This means that it keeps changing and developing as we change and develop, accompanying and shadowing us as we go through life, always bidding to make sense of our experience as far as it can on our behalf. Should we be unfortunate enough to suffer a stroke, in which selected areas of the brain may be damaged or even shut down, the brain is sometimes capable of switching on emergency procedures, taking strategic decisions to reallocate the affected functions to other brain areas. How does it do this?!

Since it does all this in biochemical code, moreover, this means that it changes physically, mirroring in an ultimately material form something which to us seems mysteriously immaterial, our experience of life. Any attempt to make sense of all this can leave us in the end with a sense of frustration – human reason, after all, is linear, one thing at a time, whereas the human brain seems to be the ultimate multitasker. It's as if they speak different languages.

The anterior insula is a small area deep in the underside of the cortex, perhaps the size of a computer mouse or a bar of soap. Amongst the roles with which it is associated are consciousness, interpersonal experience, emotion, motor control and cognitive functioning – the whole business of understanding. Not content with all that, it is also involved in our awareness of music, laughter and tears, empathy and compassion, and language! Precisely how, by means of which biochemical instructions, does it actually keep on top of these daunting tasks simultaneously, on a continuing basis? Don't ask. There is simply no way that we can keep up with this extraordinary agency within us. And our wonder at this is redoubled when we realise that this small brain sub-organ also creates for us our very sense of self, the sensation of being who we are. We know this from casework in which damage to this area can lead, for the poor individual concerned, to a loss of any sense of self.

And yet the brain, too, can come up against its own limits – for all its remarkable power, the reality it is trying to catch and express back to us is often just too subtle and elusive to express in words. This is why our language and our reason catch some things and miss others. Perhaps this may be why physicists, applying reason to the world they encounter, can come up against contradictions and limits.

Perhaps despite all its sophistication and complexity, language is essentially limited and practical, and the human reality which it catches is therefore limited and practical in the same way. Perhaps it is human language which sets the limits for what we call objective material reality.

Whatever this is all in aid of, in evolutionary terms this spectacular, mysterious faculty of understanding has certainly been a game-changer but an ambivalent one, granting to our species a lordly power over the earth without any truly mature grasp of what this power might be used for, or what on earth the point of it all might be. Through all this, however, the evolutionary logic by which human understanding emerged into history is presumably still being played out today. At this point in our history, in fact, we do seem to have arrived at a significant moment in our evolution, as our species threatens to damage the biological basis of its own future existence.

What controls the controls?

There is plentiful evidence that in many situations we experience in daily life the body on its own knows what needs to be done. People talk of the wisdom of the body. Take any accident in which injury is sustained, for example. People are aware that the body can instantaneously switch into a mode we know as shock, and that in this state, hands and feet feel cold. This is because the body has prioritised blood supplies to the key organs, in the torso and head. This mechanism is probably exceedingly ancient, emerging a very long while before anything resembling an intelligent brain had developed. This is just one example of what you could call a preconscious knowledge base, something which is shared by many species. Clearly it reacts instantaneously because speed is often critical to survival. If the reaction had to pass through intelligent consciousness it would certainly be slower, often with fatal consequences. Conscious intelligence, then, is a late development, a specialist function, evidently useful for some situations, but not for others.

Yet the great majority of brain routines in fact have nothing to do with consciousness. They are devoted quite simply to managing and sustaining the body, much of it from moment to moment, all very humdrum and routine, governing the detailed workings of every organ in its place, but also supervising and as we might say tweaking the longer-term management of the body, including the processes of birth, growth, ageing, decline and death. Every last detail of every organ or muscle or cartilage or nervous fibre is likewise kept in operation second by second, it seems, by a collaborative system in which the brain plays a crucial role. For many purposes the brain is assisted by a number of autonomous routines in various parts of the body, for example the shock routine just mentioned. The brain also maintains a similar interaction with the genes in DNA coding, always available inside the nucleus of cells. The cells respond to generic orders from the brain, and their responses, as we have seen, are impressively complex in themselves. So there is evidently a high degree of interaction between cells at the local level, steered to some extent by the brain but also involving substantial degrees of local autonomic interaction. The choreography of all this is so byzantine we cannot really say that any one agent controls or specifies anything in any direct, simple manner. It would be closer to the truth to simply say that the body and brain control the body and brain. Life, it seems, not only assembled itself from the moment of conception, it also manages itself in every possible detail from start to finish.

This degree of intricacy is the end product, moreover, of a process which has been continuously developing over hundreds of millions of years from simpler models. The human brain has something in the range of 100 billion neurons, that is 10 to the power 11. The brain of a field mouse, for example, has 10 to the power 8 neurons, just a hundred million, while a fruit fly has a hundred thousand neurons, ten to the power 5. In other words, the brains of many, many species of multi-celled creatures, field mice, fruit flies and the rest, are each a wonder of complex control, and all of this is the inheritance of very much simpler evolutionary origins. The human version of this is quite a bit more complex, but clearly one of the same kind, the same design idea.

So the controller runs the controller. When we think this

through, and consider that it is all done ultimately by means of biochemical mechanisms which have evolved in some sense by chance, it does seem likely that the actual instructions given out, whether by the brain or by the cell nucleus DNA, might well be coding only for the most generic of instructions. This might mean instructions for the making, or speeding up, or slowing down, or modifying in any one of a hundred ways of the making of certain other chemicals, which in turn... the story could often go through many, many further stages before a resulting change in, say, body shape or functioning is actually effected.

If we really stop and reflect on this, though, it would seem to be at first sight simply impossible for the brain on its own to encode every last detail of the body and keep it monitored and adjusted second by second. Some would argue that the sheer size of an ongoing task like this would be so huge that it is hard to see how even a marvel of complexity like the human brain could actually achieve it.

Occasionally there does appear to be a gene (or perhaps a gene cluster) which results in, say, a particular eye colour or a specific genetic condition, like cystic fibrosis for example, but these are rare exceptions. We also do know that there are fairly precise brain areas which are important for this or that, for example short-term memory or visual processing, say, but these are only part of a larger, infinitely more intricate, choreographed working system. More characteristically the interaction of brain, local autonomic routines, and genes in the cells can activate whole chains of reactions, maintaining a veritable dance of life in every corner of our being. The brain and the genome play key coordinating roles in this perpetual dance, but much of the detail can presumably only be determined at a more local level. Much of the time the body runs itself, and the sheer complexity of how it does this is baffling.

This is where the entire debate between nature and nurture

misses a crucial point. One argues that we are in effect the servants of our genes, the other that most of the time we merely respond to outside influences on us. In typical human logic, always looking for simplicity, we are reduced and oversimplified. Both the nature and nurture arguments express a degree of truth, but miss the wonder of our utterly baffling complexity. Human beings, it seems, need simple explanations, but this world is far from simple. Perhaps the most we can say on the nature versus nurture question is that we are programmed to make decisions, to choose, and perhaps this means that we may be on occasion programmed to be free.

Here we are with paradox again, presenting us with two elucidations of reality which appear to contradict one another. On the one hand it makes no sense to deny the reality of human freedom. To do this would undermine the whole meaning of human interaction and reduce it to nonsense. On the other hand, we can see from live brain scans that all human decisions are preceded, milliseconds before, by neural operations which appear to direct our decision, informing us a few milliseconds later and giving us the firm impression that we, the conscious agent, have made the decision. So at the level of neural functioning it appears that there is no freedom and no decision. Perhaps, however, we are more than the sum of our parts. It appears, indeed, that these very parts actually generate the whole immensely interactive world of human reality and experience. And although it is generated from within us, it is not one bit the less real. This reality, moreover, encompasses not only everyday life but also morality, law, politics, history and much besides. Not least, it encompasses the whole panoply of the scientific investigation of our material world.

So it appears that we are frequently in danger of oversimplifying our picture. This is perhaps both a weakness and a strength of human reason. The brain, it appears, is of such prolific complexity that it can be misleading to compare it to anything else, a digital computer for example. The brain, it appears, is designed to make possible 'real' decisions made by 'real' conscious agents. That is its point. Another product, or should we say by-product, is to create 'real' understanding of a 'real' world. Whole squadrons of neurons instantaneously set a pattern which creates the 'reality' of making a decision, or the 'reality' of understanding an aspect of our universe. The decision or the understanding can then turn out to be a success or a mistake, and this can affect future decisions, self-confidence, the quality of intimate relationships, or whatever else. It is all woven into the experience of life. That is where its reality resides. At one level we are dealing with purest delusion, something created inside us, at another level a real person is making a real decision or a real discovery. In a curious echo of quantum physics, we may need to keep open both points of view. 'We' exercise free will, but at the same time 'we' and our reality are created, so to speak, from inside us.

The marvel of the brain and its complex dynamics has in recent years been confirmed by live brain scans. Dramatically they demonstrate that virtually every activity, be it a perception, memory or motor response, can involve a galaxy of centres of activity lighting up, instantaneously coordinated across different sectors and sub-organs of the brain. This simultaneous choreography across the entire apparatus is evidently one of the keynotes of all brain activity. The experience of a 'me' and of 'my' reality, perpetually kept up-to-date, is perhaps one of the more celebrated outcomes of this. The process of reasoning, making some sense out of this cavalcade of experience, is another. Indeed the one is part of the other. Within the brain itself, making sense of the world is closely entwined with making sense of 'me', and making sense of my making sense. The circuits, it seems, are interconnected.

A hunger to make sense

Every time we remember something, a mechanism inside us refreshes it, making it more vivid and easier to remember in the future. But quite often it also re-edits it, perhaps changing one or two key words, perhaps trimming out the odd detail. Distance alters the view. Over an expanse of time the importance of some things can really stand out, while others simply fade from view. So somewhere inside us, presumably, there has to be a memory re-editing programme, in turn part of a wider programme which makes sense of our changing world.

Memory, then, is about meaning, searching for it, adding definition to it, and updating it as times change. So our entire experience of life, and the meaning it has for us, is recorded in its simply immense detail inside our heads. Clearly this process is more creative and more complex than we can easily imagine.

The synapse across which an electrical message can pass from one neuron to another is, we are told, like a threshold. Our brain is checking out reality, making sense of what it receives, all the while, and the conscious mind is much of the time largely unaware of this. Indeed our brain operates much faster than our conscious mind could ever keep up with.

It takes an organ of truly fabulous complexity to enable us to half remember things, or to have a name on the tip of our tongue, or to have forebodings in dreams which we cannot pinpoint, or to be surprised by a sudden Eureka moment which seems to have come from nowhere, or to be unexpectedly moved to tears by a symphony. Come to think of it, it takes an equally rare complexity to search for a meaning which can make sense of our entire experience, including our entire reality, our inner universe.

Today robotic machines are being developed at a rapid pace. There is already talk of the machines taking power by stealth, seductively looking after our welfare, little by little taking charge of our future, and this could indeed be one of the major challenges of our century. At the same time, though, this new relationship with artificial intelligence may hold up a foil to us, highlighting the distinctive, contrary, creative quality of our own inborn, evolved intelligence. In the end these machines may eventually help us to better understand human understanding itself – and who knows, we might need this enhanced understanding as we go through challenging times.

Suddenly all this can seem like an unaccountable gift to us, working away twenty-four hours a day, waking or sleeping, every millisecond of our lives, but we scarcely ever give it a passing thought. Yet this drive to make sense of things, this urge to understand our surrounding reality can fulfil us and satisfy us like nothing else can. And this inborn drive lies at the very heart of the evolutionary inheritance of our species. Understanding defines who we are.

We are fabulously complex, unpredictable, miraculous creatures, moving forward through time, true children of this creation. And, once this realisation has hit us, once we have picked ourselves up off the floor, the experience of understanding this can give an authentic zip and a zest to the experience of being alive. Understanding is a special kind of magic. It can transform our world, and it can transform us. Perhaps we need to celebrate it more, with real gusto and enthusiasm. Anyone care to dance?

Chapter 12

(Re?)creating the creation

A framework for understanding

In recent years we have come to recognise that many species have an impressive degree of working intelligence, something which we had previously underrated. A degree of intelligence after all creates a significant edge in the competition for survival, and is therefore to be found in varying concentrations in many species.

A distinctively human intelligence has a long pedigree, elements of the groundwork being laid down among prehuman forebears as far back as 7–12 million years ago, in an era characterised by competition between different species of intelligent apes. It then came together during the time of Homo erectus between one and two million years ago. Perhaps more decisive, however, was the much more recent emergence of Homo sapiens in Africa around a mere two hundred thousand years ago.

This new intelligence carried quite distinctive consequences. It created a unique hunger for understanding, something which could bring a new degree of security in a still dangerous world. Along with the new understanding, though, came a more sensitive, more powerful imagination and a long, vulnerable childhood, so fear, too, became more intelligent and more vivid, and this made the desire for security still more urgent. Understanding became a great, generic antidote to fear, and soon it became a dominant factor in sexual selection.

In today's very different world this hunger for understanding still defines us as a species. Amid all the affluence, greed, violence, and insecurity reflected in much of current politics, humanity still cherishes a widespread aspiration for understanding. Not only can this bring material reward, status and respect, today it is also unmistakably its own reward. This is true pre-eminently of the remarkable worldwide phenomenon of modern science.

In the last chapter we explored some biological foundations of human consciousness and reasoning. In the chapter before that we looked at its deep practical foundations in early human prehistory, rooted in the necessities of day-to-day survival. All this in time produced human language, with its innovative framework of grammatical understanding.

So when physicists today ask whether light is a particle or a wave, they demonstrate the nature and the limits of the human language they are using. The words particle and wave were necessarily borrowed from practical daily life, a particle being small and hard like a grain of sand perhaps; a wave behaving more like the waves of a liquid, like sea water. Both, however, are nouns, and are therefore seen to some degree as independent, separate entities, creating a need to explain how they interact with each other. The idea of a law, meanwhile, comes from a very different social activity, and the idea of a mechanism conjures up the picture of some kind of contrivance or machine, presumably devised and made by a craftsman – metaphors are everywhere in human language.

Perhaps above all, as we also discovered, language is linear and is designed to deal with one thing at a time. The unconscious brain, however, like the great universe itself, is an impressive multitasker, everything going about its business simultaneously. The best we can do is take one thing at a time, and keep in mind that that is what our language requires us to do. So in different ways our language both liberates and imprisons us.

This framework of understanding is kept in place, then, by a set of working grammatical rules, and all of this, moreover, is part of the instinctive inheritance acquired in the process of our evolution. This means that our instinct for language is not derived from recent experience. On the contrary, it is the framework which we bring to experience, by means of which we make sense of experience. The 18th century German philosopher Immanuel Kant would have said it is a priori, or as we might say today, it is wired into us. Without some framework of assumptions by which we can structure our experiences, they wouldn't make very much sense at all.

The achievements of the sciences are indeed immense but very recent. Our language goes back much further, and the human need for a sense of reality very much further again. So the sciences, in responding to an ancient human need, seem to be stuck with the preset limits of human language.

But our understanding makes other assumptions too, beyond just the rules of grammar. For example it tends to assume a universally applicable cause and effect. Our world is impenetrably complex, but human cause and effect is fundamentally understood in a greatly simplified model, like billiard balls – a causes b, which in turn impacts on c and d. Meanwhile an assumed universality of cause and effect in turn assumes a universal extension of space and time. As we have seen, this has created problems and paradoxes in cosmology.

This framework also assumes certain rules of logic and of arithmetic, and in time developed the entire world of mathematics, which is so central to the modern scientific quest for reality. As a previous chapter concluded, mathematics sometimes seems to have an almost coercive power over us – we feel we cannot argue with its results.

At the same time numbers can lead us to strange places. Exceedingly large numbers are one thing, and mathematicians are used to them. Our universe is characterised on all sides by exceedingly large numbers. Infinity, on the other hand, hovers in the background as we attempt to make sense of our reality, for example in the speculation about countless other universes in a so-called multiverse. Huge numbers follow ultimately logical rules, and infinity is part of mathematics, but infinity seems to have at best a controversial place in our understanding of the universe. Our instinctive framework of understanding apparently does not extend to infinity. Perhaps it wasn't designed for that.

But perhaps the most pervasive assumption in this framework of reality is indicated by the single-lettered pronoun 'I'. Our language framework assumes a solid, straightforward, separate entity which is experiencing all this. So it is easy to assume that this 'I' is solid and straightforward, even in the face of plentiful evidence that it is created and maintained by the brain, is unimaginably complex, and is interconnected to our universe at countless levels and in endless details. At the same time it surely makes no sense to say this 'I' is an illusion. It too is wired into us, all part of an instinctive framework of assumptions which generates a quintessentially human reality.

Behind the logic of science

The development of the sciences during the last few centuries represents arguably one of the few truly important, truly pivotal turning points in the entire span of human history. Perhaps the only other development to which it can be compared would be the much earlier development of language itself. These two achievements, language and science, both answer the urgent need to understand our world and our place in it, a need built in to our evolution as highly intelligent and therefore insecure creatures.

Time after time in history, discoveries in the sciences have transformed the way we see our world and this has transformed how we see ourselves. The insights of Newton, Darwin and Einstein each awakened us to a new way of seeing ourselves in our surroundings, a way which no one had previously even imagined. In a similar way the insights of the 18th century astronomers and the early geologists of the late 18th and early 19th centuries profoundly changed our understanding of the age and the scale of things, and the work of chemists from Lavoisier to Mendeleev revealed the fundamental order within the fundamental elements of matter. By the early 20th century the fierce, strange world within the atom itself was revealed, while Hubble and his colleagues revealed the awesome age and size of the entire creation. Further discoveries have accumulated at a giddy pace especially in the past few decades.

Of course the emerging picture in its endless detail can bowl us over. The thing is, though, the picture itself has meanwhile changed, and not just in its mass of detail. As discoveries race ahead in different fields, more of the gaps are being filled in. Where we once saw separate fields of discovery, we can now see a single connected fabric, and this is giving us a new vision of the whole thing.

How will this in the end affect us? When we contemplate the cumulative impact of this new vision, it does seem pretty unlikely that it will have just no particular consequences for us. Surely it cannot fail to change us in the century or two ahead, although it may very likely do so in ways which we cannot for the moment foresee. Our century is in any case likely to be full of bewildering change, but perhaps amid all this there may be grounds for a careful optimism. Perhaps we may find ourselves fulfilling the potential of our own evolution, already laid down in the long millennia of our prehistory, and perhaps the key to this potential will be a creative understanding, pointing the way. Guided by this inherited wisdom, we might then begin to understand where we are headed and who we might become. It wouldn't be the first time humans had been inspired by new understanding.

Major breakthroughs in the sciences have often come as a result of true leaps of the imagination, seeing new possibilities no one had seen before. These possibilities didn't come from nowhere – Newton spoke of standing on the shoulders of giants. But what lay behind the new breakthroughs? Consciously or not, the discoverer was essentially looking for simplicity, an ability to explain more with less. The evidence often followed later.

Simplicity, order, pattern, discerned within an overwhelmingly deep complexity – this is the paradoxical framework of a human reality, wired in to us just as surely as grammar and numbers, cause and effect, time and space.

All that is?

How can we possibly sum up our entire surrounding reality? Is there a word, a single word, which can do this? The usual superlatives come to mind – awesome, breathtaking and so on. Amongst these, perhaps two words do catch something of its essence. Firstly, it is overwhelming – perhaps an obvious point and easy to miss, but nevertheless fundamental. The reality which we are encountering is uniquely overwhelming. Secondly there is nothing to which we can compare it – it is in a perfectly literal sense incomparable.

What else can we say, summing all this up? This universe is certainly friendly to our human reason. We need only list the major discoveries of the last few centuries. But this creation has seldom revealed its secrets easily. At the moments when the major, pivotal discoveries were made they were for the most part fiendishly hard to achieve, often requiring true creative leaps of understanding.

At the same time this creation is also mightily strange. Once upon a time, we are told, the entire universe had an explosive birth moment, seemingly bursting out of no space and no time at all. Yet current evidence leads us to conclude that in the last act of the drama it will fade into ever-expanding emptiness. It started with a bang, it seems, but will apparently end with not even so much as a whimper. There again, others would protest that logically this cannot be, that something with a beginning but not an ending has to be a logical absurdity.

What else? This creation is vast but not infinitely vast. It is measured out in billions of light years, yet a very specific, limited sum of billions of light years. Light, meanwhile, travels across the universe in all directions simultaneously at an unimaginable but specific speed, a speed which is intimately tied in with the fabric in which space-time and matter-energy are all held together. How wonderfully strange!

It does seem that this creation consists ultimately of inexpressible numbers of wave-particles, some of these captured within atoms in a peculiar dance we know as matter, while others act out another dance in which they are in some sense free, like light and other electromagnetic phenomena. Throughout this space-time universe wave-particles are apparently being created and destroyed all the time in one continuous, rhythmic oscillation many, many times per second. Or so it seems at this point in time.

This whole fabric is all ultimately held together by just a few overarching forces – gravity, an electromagnetic force, and two so-called strong and weak intra-atomic forces. There has been progress in integrating some of these forces, but not all of them. But in any case why do these forces operate at the specific strength they do? We think that if even one of them had been set at a different strength, this particular universe might never have come into existence, but we don't really understand why this should be so.

All this, matter and light and much besides, emerges (if that is the right word) from an extremely microscopic world within the wave-particles. At a level some way beneath even this submicroscopic world, rational investigation soon becomes problematic and if you keep on going down to ever tinier dimensions it apparently becomes impossible. Likewise, at scales of vastness measured at, say, many trillions of trillions of light years, human reason seems to fade into nothing. Although it seems odd to say so, human rationality appears to be designed to work within certain limits of scale – vast but quite clearly finite. But again, in the future this view may be superseded. Science, it seems, will always be open-ended.

Meanwhile, in a similar way, the universe is so impenetrably complex that beyond a certain level of detail it likewise appears to be in practice unknowable. Yet out of this vast ocean of impenetrable complexity, simplicity, pattern and a rationally ordered reality nevertheless do emerge. Given this, the fact that this actually happens is perhaps the oddest thing about it.

And from this material world can sometimes emerge the intricate world of life, a rhythmic electrochemical dance operating at and around the gates of the living cell. Is it too much to see a degree of natural kinship between the material world and the world of living things – both involving some degree of ultimately electrical activity?

And in the world of living creatures a degree of practical intelligence is relatively common, and from this has emerged the whole human sense of reality, the true miracle (if you'll pardon the expression) of an inner universe within us.

So it appears that the world of living things is not a living spark in a dead universe. On the contrary, it does seem to be a natural product, rare no doubt, but nevertheless a spontaneous outcome of an electromagnetic, space-time creation. This creation, moreover, evolves in its own way just as surely as the living world evolves.

Finally this universe, being deeply complex, is also open-ended, always open to new possibilities. In this too we resemble it.

In the end we have to say that this whole thing is on several counts thoroughly improbable. Yet it exists. Likewise we ourselves are thoroughly improbable, yet here we are, magnificently alive, trying to work it all out.

A single fabric

Once the sum of human knowledge of our world was like an archipelago of different islands of understanding, surrounded by great seas of unexplained territory, like early maps of the earth. Today we can speak of a single map. People today speak of the universe as a single fabric, weaving together space, time, energy and matter. Moreover this two hundred billion galaxy creation, it turns out, on occasion produces life and then intelligent life perfectly naturally. We ourselves, then, and our questing curiosity, are part of this single fabric.

The unimaginable vastness of this universe, examined in Chapter 1, does matter here. At first we may think that something which has the truly endless complexity of life on earth surely could never repeat itself. Never ever. But at the scale of our many billion galaxy universe the most unlikely things become possible. Vast scale, you could say, can conjure things which at a more local level seem vanishingly improbable. A statement like this seems counter-intuitive, but perhaps we have got used to this kind of thing by now.

So we need no longer picture ourselves as intruders wandering through an alien place. We can now see that we belong here, woven into it indeed in a thousand details at a thousand levels.

Our understanding of understanding itself has likewise changed. Human understanding has evolved from simpler roots deep in our prehistory. Today this understanding is at the very heart of our genetic and behavioural inheritance, enabling us to respond with high creativity in challenging times. That is why it has evolved.

Is the material universe truly all that exists? There are those who say so. According to this view, everything else – history, politics, morality, religion, art, literature – is 'only' an aspect, or a consequence, or a by-product, of human nature. Certainly in modern culture there is a widespread unspoken assumption that scientific truth is in the end more real than all the other sources of truth.

Science, however, with all its dazzling successes, is an expression of human nature every bit as much as all the other sources of knowledge. It's not just that – remarkably enough – we reflect this universe in biochemical code inside our brain. It's also the fact that human language and human reasoning express an ancient, fundamental human need to do this, to understand our surroundings in our own grammatical, linguistic way. But to understand something is in a sense to recreate it. This need to understand and thereby to recreate this creation, this is in our bones.

This universe, then, is in a special sense acutely, profoundly ambiguous. On the one hand it is splendidly 'out there', objectively real, and this reality out-scales us, yet on the other hand it is we, following our own instinctive needs, who have made it real. Making it real, moreover, is more than just a matter of grammar – behind that is a biochemical, material reality. Remarkably, our sense of reality is created, stored and continuously updated in a physical, molecular code, part of the material world, inside our heads. It is easy to forget how astonishing this is.

Let's say this again. Out of a maze of biochemical networking we routinely create not just the miracle of human conscious experience but also an entire interior universe. Bizarrely, our universe, then, exists simultaneously in two models, one 'out there', the other within us. What's more, both models are valid. Each of our two universes is part of the other. How strange is that?

Perhaps we thought the universe would be like a rational calculus machine, yet it has turned out to be more like an ecstatic, magical dance. We thought that we humans were wandering aimlessly in space, unaccountably set down into an alien world, whereas we turned out to have arisen out of it, intimately woven from its fabric.

In the end the whole thing has a strange, magical quality, hard to put into words. In an earlier chapter we noticed that every passing moment of time is unique and will never be repeated. Isn't this also true of the entire universe? This too is unique, utterly unique and will never be repeated.

Does this universe, this encircling reality, express a meaning for us? Perhaps not in the clunky way of simple, one-plus-one logic, but nevertheless it does speak to us unmistakably in its own way. This universe bristles, vibrates with ceaseless energy, expressing a glory, beauty and mystery which together can powerfully affect us, sweeping us along, awestruck, taking us well beyond our habitual obsession with ourselves. This is a distinctive kind of meaning which unforgettably blends rationality with a never-ceasing energy and a stunning, luring, altogether captivating beauty.

An adaptive inheritance

It is all so easy to forget just how splendidly equipped we are to investigate and understand this surrounding reality. Our evolution, it appears, has prepared us in precise detail for a distinctively human way of understanding. This is part of our evolutionary inheritance, still echoing down to us from our long prehistory.

When we finally come to understand something, we experience an unmistakable sense of recognition, a little bit like remembering a name we had forgotten. It feels right. It's as if we are contacting circuits which are already set up for this, something which is in a sense born in us. And this moment of recognition is the reward we were instinctively looking for. Understanding our world not only brings us a degree of security – it also inspires us, and we are inspired partly because we are in some sense liberated, taken out of ourselves. All this can give us a zest for life. It all fits together.

The thing is, we sometimes seem to be frustrated, even in some degree distressed, when we fail to understand ourselves and our world. So many people go through life seemingly in this state of underlying frustration, living lives (in the memorable phrase) of quiet desperation. When people cannot make any sense of themselves, they naturally look elsewhere for reassurance. Is it possible that human greed, insecurity and violence, responding to a deep-rooted underlying anxiety, may be in part an outcome of not understanding who we are? But if humanity were to find a way of understanding itself which took full account of what we now know, then who knows what might follow? It wouldn't be the first time we humans have re-imagined our world and ourselves within it. This seems to be a periodically recurring feature of human history. It even looks as if we may be naturally quite good at it!

The times we live in are certainly ambiguous, full of both menace and hope. Medical advances in the last century or two have created a colossal population bubble. In just the last half-century biological discoveries have awakened public opinion to the lethal damage we are all the while doing to the earth and ultimately to ourselves. Meanwhile living standards are rising right across the world, creating for many millions a new wave of what we might call naïve first-time affluence, while the world, remarkably, totters towards one single world community for the very first time in history. Mass education and a giddily developing technology, as we know, are shrinking the world from year to year. We live amid looming challenges and remarkable new insights.

Can we fit the new insights together to steer safely through the challenges? As we think about this, we realise that our children are looking on. We might well wonder what they and their children will make of all this, and make of us, looking back. That's if they survive.

If we continue to see ourselves in isolation from our surrounding creation, as if it had nothing to do with us, then human life may well appear to be utterly insignificant and in the end pointless. But as our understanding of this new world sinks in, this old point of view may begin to look outdated and may well start to fade. From what we now know the story of our deep origins is quite simply more magnificent than any of us could ever have imagined, we on our little pearl of a planet, our own craft, all the while spinning somewhere through deep space.

This astonishing creation is where we came from and where we are at home, living out our span. In due course, like all creatures, we will pass away, but the great universe will live on, in all its splendour, for many billions of years after we have gone. We know that it was telling its endlessly astounding tale eons before the first humans were ever there to hear it. This creation, then, our origin and our destination, can inspire us as nothing else can, a standing antidote to our ego-obsessed little lives. And this too is part of our inheritance.

Perhaps to our own surprise, we have actually captured this extraordinary creation; like true hunters we have caught it with the net of our understanding. Now it's as if we are invited to do more than just witness this spectacle and make sense of it, but to find a way to respond to it with care and intelligence. This, then, can give us back a human agenda, a new role, or perhaps rather an ancient, newly rediscovered role, placing us back at the centre of our creation as we understand it.

Who knows how this new understanding of ours will actually change the direction of human history? The present century's increasingly global perspective and its growing preoccupation with climate change and longer-term sustainability is a promising start. As I write this, people are already saying that the petrol engine will be superseded within thirty years and that in the second half of the century there could well be a radical decline in meat consumption. Meanwhile the cost of renewable energy is plummeting month by month.

Nuancing or modifying the underlying politics of greed, fear and violence, on the other hand, looks likely to be an altogether larger challenge. Is it too much to hope that at some time in the middle future this interlocking complex of greed and insecurity will finally be seen as a suicidal delusion menacing all that we value, something to be despised and kept warily at arm's length? Perhaps it's just too early to say. Immense changes are no doubt already underway, in our world and also within us as we stumble through this century.

Could a new era of understanding provide the key to the next stage of human evolution? Who knows? – Homo sapiens could yet have a long history ahead, and much to achieve. At this moment as we peer into the future, we dare not predict, but there may be reasons to hope.

Taking wing!

Recently an astronomer reported investigating the light from an early star, estimated at 12 billion light years or so distance. The light from this star, he realised, had set out before there was a Milky Way galaxy, and had already travelled nearly two-thirds of its journey towards us before our solar system had formed.

Despite everything, we may still feel that we haven't done full justice to the fabulous creation which has brought us to being. Perhaps we need to try for one more final response, aware that the plodding logic of prose has perhaps missed something. At this point maybe we need to let our words take wing!

It's the ubiquitous, universal energy which in the end might capture our attention and our admiration, an unquenchable energy displayed on all sides, everywhere and always dancing, dancing, creating newness, freshness, youth to the end of time. There are all kinds of dances, small and large, fast and slow, dances within dances within dances, exquisitely intricate dances within the living cell and slow majestic dances among the galaxies. This universe teems with a creative energy, apparently effortless, far outpacing former ideas of magic and the supernatural.

Yet the birth moment which inaugurated all this, this moment which still passes all understanding, has a combination of unimaginable power and unfathomable mystery. One day we might understand it better, but even in a confidently rational world it still richly deserves to be called magical.

Being unimaginably vast, however, is just the start of it. Since it is also so deeply complex and endlessly open-ended, it is hard to see how the quest to investigate it could ever come to a definitive conclusion.

Out of an ocean of unfathomable complexity order and simplicity are somehow conjured into existence. From that order on occasion the still deeper complexity of a living world can arise, and from that in turn the truly miraculous reality of perfectly ordinary human experience. All this is part of one fabric, but nested, one world inside another, like a Russian doll. And in humanity, and in all intelligent life forms like us, it's as if this whole creation has become in some degree aware of itself.

Could we ever imagine a more creative explosion of beauty and energy, a more hugely positive statement? It appears to have been created, magicked out of nothing, simply to express the sheer zest of its own exuberant existence. The dance celebrates the dance. As a Hindu text has it, this creation was conceived in joy.

This universe can move us in all kinds of ways. It can fire us with exhilaration, can overcome us with awe, can lure us onward with its startling beauty, and can still send a shiver of something like panic down the spine. But perhaps above all it moves us in a very particularly human way. We are invited to witness this wonder, and returning the compliment we find ourselves setting out on a quest to understand it. Ultimately, then, this can seem like an intimate symbiotic relationship between us and it, between these inquisitive, nervous creatures, as if just awakened from a long sleep, and the fabulous creation which has brought them to being.

We finish this quest with something like a story, but the logic of this story is not linear, like our human logic, but multidimensional. Moreover, in this quest to investigate and understand it, to plumb its depths, we have at no point reached rock bottom, at no point have we managed to find some final principle, or some equation or algorithm which could conclusively sum it all up. Instead we have come round in a circle, back to ourselves, back to human instincts. So we rediscover ourselves, open-ended creatures engaging in an open-ended quest in an open-ended universe.

We also finish with an experience. Consider this extraordinary combination of dazzling glory, sheer size, fathomless mystery and the unaccountable privilege of witnessing it all. This can engender in us a fizzing cocktail of emotions, among them exhilaration and joy, an experience of understanding and of transcendence we can call ecstatic. Mere words will probably sound banal from here on, failing entirely to convey the fullness of what we might want to say.

Words, then, eventually peter out without a final answer. We keep trying to shoehorn our universe to fit our words, and words are all we have, but sooner or later they stutter to a halt. But this, precisely this, has surely been worth finding out! Besides, this hardly leaves us with a sense of disappointment. Quite the contrary, our voyage surely leaves us simply open-mouthed with admiration, humbled by what we have encountered.

Which is the more astonishing? The sheer size of things, from the vastness of the 200 billion galaxies, to the unimaginable dimensions deep within the particles which make up the atom? Which is the more remarkable, the sheer size of all this, or its deep, fathomless complexity?

Which is the more impressive? The truly byzantine complexity of living tissue, or the wondrous pinnacle of human consciousness, creating its own inner universe, or the blind processes of evolution, by means of which all the phenomena of life have arisen, originally out of non-living matter?

Which is the more baffling? The condensation of this entire material universe from constituent wave-particles of energy? – or the emergence of these wave-particles from, well, from the unknown worlds from which they arose?

On reflection, which is the more surprising? The fact that this creation is endlessly open-ended and unpredictable in its fine detail, or the fact that at the same time, in and through its complexity, a rational order can be found?

However we answer these riddles, we ourselves will never be the same again. Our new understanding cannot help but change us. After all, we are made to understand. It's in our genes, in our evolutionary inheritance.

Like the processes of science, this book has left us with more and more questions, an endless stream of questions. It also leaves us in jaw-dropping wonder, and this wonder doesn't feel as if it is about to dry up. It takes us right out of ourselves, beyond our human limitations. It feels timeless.

I rejoice in the knowledge of my biological uniqueness, and my biological antiquity, and my biological kinship with all other forms of life.
This knowledge roots me.
Oliver Sacks

List of sources

Diane Ackerman. *An Alchemy of Mind: The Marvel and Mystery of the Brain.* Scribner, 2004

Douglas Adams. *The Restaurant at the End of the Universe.* Pan Books, 1980

Jim Al-Khalili and Johnjoe McFadden. *Life on the Edge: The Coming of Age of Quantum Biology.* Black Swan, 2015

Frances Ashcroft. *The Spark of Life: Electricity in the Human Body.* Penguin, 2013

Isaac Asimov. *The Chemicals of Life.* Signet, 1954

Peter Atkins. *The Periodic Kingdom.* Phoenix, 1995

David Attenborough. *Life on Earth: A Natural History.* Collins/BBC, 1979

Joanne Baker. *50 ideas you really need to know: Universe.* Quercus, 2010

Philip Ball. *H²O: A Biography of Water.* Phoenix, 1999

Philip Ball. *The Elements: A Very Short Introduction.* Oxford, 2002

Simon Baron-Cohen. *Zero Degrees of Empathy: A New Theory of Human Cruelty and Kindness.* Penguin, 2012

John D. Barrow. *The Infinite Book.* Vintage, 2005

David Beerling. *The Emerald Planet: How plants changed earth's history.* Oxford, 2007

Michael Braungart and William McDonough. *Cradle to Cradle.* Vintage, 2009

Michael Brooks. *The Quantum Astrologer's Handbook.* Scribe, 2017

Bill Bryson. *A Short History of Nearly Everything.* Black Swan, 2004

Mark Buchanan. *Ubiquity: The Science of History, or Why the World is Simpler Than We Think.* Phoenix, 2001

Nigel Calder. *Magic Universe: A Grand Tour of Modern Science.* Oxford, 2005

Fritjof Capra. *The Tao of Physics.* Fontana/Collins, 1975

Nessa Carey. *The Epigenetics Revolution.* Icon Books, 2011

Enrico Coen. *The Art of Genes: how organisms make themselves.* Oxford, 1999

Jack Cohen and Ian Stewart. *The Collapse of Chaos: discovering simplicity in a complex world.* Penguin, 1994

Paul Colinvaux. *Why Big Fierce Animals Are Rare.* Pelican, 1980

Patricia Daniels. *The New Solar System: Ice Worlds, Moons and Planets Redefined.* National Geographic, 2009

Daniel Richard Danielson. *The Book of the Cosmos: Imagining the Universe from Heraclitus to Hawking.* Perseus, 2000

Jamie A. Davies. *Life Unfolding: How the human body creates itself.* Oxford, 2014

Paul Davies. *The Fifth Miracle: The Search for the Origin of Life.* Penguin, 1999

Paul Davies. *The Goldilocks Enigma: Why is the Universe Just Right for Life?* Penguin, 2006

Richard Dawkins. *The Blind Watchmaker.* Penguin, 1986

Richard Dawkins. *Unweaving the Rainbow.* Penguin, 1998

Richard Dawkins. *The Ancestor's Tale: A Pilgrimage to the Dawn of Life.* Phoenix, 2004

Daniel Dennett. *Consciousness Explained.* Penguin, 1993

Keith Devlin. *The Man of Numbers: Fibonacci's Arithmetic Revolution.* Bloomsbury, 2011

Jared Diamond. *Why Is Sex Fun? The Evolution of Human Sexuality.* Phoenix, 1997

Norman Doidge. *The Brain that Changes Itself.* Penguin, 2007

Marcus du Sautoy. *What We Cannot Know.* HarperCollins, 2016

Marcus du Sautoy. *The Music of the Primes.* HarperPerennial, 2004

Robin Dunbar. *The Human Story: A New History of Mankind's Evolution.* Faber and Faber, 2004

Robin Dunbar. *How Many Friends Does One Person Need?* Faber and Faber, 2010

Stephen Emmott. *10 Billion.* Penguin, 2013

Clive Finlayson. *The Humans Who Went Extinct: Why Neanderthals died out and we survived.* Oxford, 2009

Richard Fortey. *Life: An Unauthorised Biography.* HarperCollins, 1997

Michael Frayn. *The Human Touch: Our Part in the Creation of a Universe.* Faber and Faber, 2006

Christophe Galfard. *The Universe in Your Hand.* Pan Books, 2016

Stephen Jay Gould. *Wonderful Life: The Burgess Shale and the Nature of History.* Penguin, 1989

Brian Greene. *The Fabric of the Cosmos.* Penguin, 2004

Susan Greenfield. *The Private Life of the Brain.* Penguin, 2000

John Gribbin. *Stardust: The Cosmic Recycling of Stars, Planets and People.* Penguin, 2001

John Gribbin. *Deep Simplicity: Chaos, Complexity and the Emergence of Life.* Penguin, 2005

John Gribbin. *The Universe: A Biography.* Penguin, 2006

John Gribbin. *13.8: The Quest to Find the True Age of the Universe and the Theory of Everything.* Icon Books, 2015

Rudyard Griffiths, ed. *Do Humankind's Best Days Lie Ahead?* Anansi Press, 2016

Yuval Noah Harari. *Sapiens: A Brief History of Humankind.* Penguin Random House, 2014

Yuval Noah Harari. *Homo Deus: A Brief History of Tomorrow.* Penguin Random House, 2015

Robert M. Hazen. *The Story of Earth: The First 4.5 Billion Years, from Stardust to Living Planet.* Penguin, 2012

George Johnson. *Fire in the Mind: Science, Faith, and the Search for Order.* Alfred Knopf, 1995

Steven Johnson. *Emergence: The Connected Lives of Ants, Brains, Cities and Software.* Penguin, 2001

Steve Jones. *The Language of the Genes.* HarperCollins, 1993

Steve Jones. *Almost Like a Whale: 'The Origin of Species' Updated.* Black Swan, 2001

Steve Jones. *Y: The Descent of Men.* Abacus, 2002

Marek Kohn. *As We Know It: Coming to Terms with an Evolved Mind.* Granta, 1999

James Le Fanu. *Why Us? How science rediscovered the mystery of ourselves.* Harper, 2009

Richard Lewontin. *The Triple Helix: gene, organism and environment.* Harvard, 2000

Eugene Marais. *The Soul of the White Ant.* Penguin, 1973

Henry Marsh. *Do No Harm: Stories of Life, Death and Brain Surgery.* Weidenfeld & Nicolson, 2014

Mark Maslin. *The Cradle of Humanity.* Oxford University Press, 2017

Steven Mithen. *The Prehistory of the Mind: A Search for the Origins of Art, Religion and Science.* Phoenix, 1996

Desmond Morris. *Gestures: a new look at the human animal.* Triad/ Granada, 1981

Stephen Moss. *The Robin: A Biography.* Square Peg, 2017

Ted Nield. *Supercontinent: 10 Billion Years in the Life of Our Planet.* Granta, 2007

Denis Noble. *The Music of Life: Biology Beyond Genes.* Oxford, 2006

Sherwin Nuland. *The Wisdom of the Body.* Chatto and Windus, 1997

Neil Oliver. *A History of Ancient Britain.* Phoenix, 2011

Stephen Oppenheimer. *Out of Eden: The Peopling of the World.* Constable and Robinson, 2003

Steven Pinker. *The Stuff of Thought: Language as a Window into Human Nature.* Penguin, 2008

Steven Pinker. *The Better Angels of Our Nature.* Penguin, 2011

Martin Rees. *Just Six Numbers: The Deep Forces That Shape the Universe.* Phoenix, 1999

Matt Ridley. *The Origins of Virtue: Human Instincts and the Evolution of Cooperation.* Penguin, 1996

Matt Ridley. *Genome: The Autobiography of a Species in 23 Chapters.*

Fourth Estate, 1999

Alice Roberts. *The Incredible Unlikeliness of Being: Evolution and the Making of Us.* Heron, 2014

Steven Rose. *The Making of Memory: From Molecules to Mind.* Vintage, 2003

Carlo Rovelli. *Seven Brief Lessons on Physics.* Allen Lane, 2014

Carlo Rovelli. *Reality Is Not What It Seems.* Allen Lane, 2016

Adam Rutherford. *Creation: The Origin of Life/The Future of Life.* Penguin, 2014

Oliver Sacks. *Seeing Voices.* Picador, 1989

Oliver Sacks. *The River of Consciousness.* Alfred A. Knopf, 2017

Caleb Scharf. *Gravity's Engines: The Other Side of Black Holes.* Penguin, 2013

Caleb Scharf. *The Copernicus Complex: The Quest for Our Cosmic (In)Significance.* Penguin, 2015

James Shreeve. *The Neandertal Enigma: Solving the Mystery of Modern Human Origins.* Penguin, 1995

Neil Shubin. *Your Inner Fish: The amazing discovery of our 375-million-year-old ancestor.* Penguin, 2008

Mark Stevenson. *An Optimist's Tour of the Future.* Profile, 2011

Ian Stewart. *Nature's Numbers: Discovering Order and Pattern in the Universe.* Weidenfeld & Nicolson, 1995

Ian Stewart. *Why Beauty Is Truth: A History of Symmetry.* Basic Books, 2008

Rebecca Stott. *Darwin's Ghosts: In Search of the First Evolutionists.* Bloomsbury, 2012

Chris Stringer. *The Origin of Our Species.* Penguin, 2011

Brian Swimme. *The Universe is a Green Dragon: A Cosmic Creation Story.* Bear and Co., 1984

Brian Swimme and Thomas Berry. *The Universe Story.* HarperSanFrancisco, 1992

Jill Bolte Taylor. *My Stroke of Insight: A Brain Scientist's Personal Journey.* Plume, 2009

Peter Toghill. *The Geology of Britain: An Introduction.* Crowood

Press, 2000

Neil Turok. *The Universe Within: From Quantum to Cosmos.* Anansi, 2012

Ian Vince. *The Lie of the Land: An under-the-field guide to the British Isles.* Boxtree/Macmillan, 2010

Peter D. Ward. *Under a Green Sky: Global Warming, the Mass Extinctions of the Past, and What They Can Tell Us About Our Future.* Smithsonian, 2007

Robert Winston. *The Human Mind: And How to Make the Most of It.* Bantam, 2003

Peter Wohlleben. *The Hidden Life of Trees.* Random House, 2015

Andrea Wulf. *The Invention of Nature: The Adventures of Alexander von Humboldt, The Lost Hero of Science.* John Murray, 2015

ACADEMIC AND SPECIALIST

Iff Books publishes non-fiction. It aims to work with authors and titles that augment our understanding of the human condition, society and civilisation, and the world or universe in which we live.
If you have enjoyed this book, why not tell other readers by posting a review on your preferred book site.
Recent bestsellers from Iff Books are:

Why Materialism Is Baloney
How true skeptics know there is no death and fathom answers to life, the universe, and everything
Bernardo Kastrup
A hard-nosed, logical, and skeptic non-materialist metaphysics, according to which the body is in mind, not mind in the body.
Paperback: 978-1-78279-362-5 ebook: 978-1-78279-361-8

The Fall
Steve Taylor
The Fall discusses human achievement versus the issues of war, patriarchy and social inequality.
Paperback: 978-1-78535-804-3 ebook: 978-1-78535-805-0

Brief Peeks Beyond
Critical essays on metaphysics, neuroscience, free will, skepticism and culture
Bernardo Kastrup
An incisive, original, compelling alternative to current mainstream cultural views and assumptions.
Paperback: 978-1-78535-018-4 ebook: 978-1-78535-019-1

Framespotting
Changing how you look at things changes how
you see them
Laurence & Alison Matthews
A punchy, upbeat guide to framespotting. Spot deceptions and
hidden assumptions; swap growth for growing up. See and be free.
Paperback: 978-1-78279-689-3 ebook: 978-1-78279-822-4

Is There an Afterlife?
David Fontana
Is there an Afterlife? If so what is it like? How do Western ideas
of the afterlife compare with Eastern? David Fontana presents
the historical and contemporary evidence for survival of physical
death.
Paperback: 978-1-90381-690-5

Nothing Matters
a book about nothing
Ronald Green
Thinking about Nothing opens the world to everything by
illuminating new angles to old problems and stimulating new
ways of thinking.
Paperback: 978-1-84694-707-0 ebook: 978-1-78099-016-3

Panpsychism
The Philosophy of the Sensuous Cosmos
Peter Ells
Are free will and mind chimeras? This book, anti-materialistic
but respecting science, answers: No! Mind is foundational to all
existence.
Paperback: 978-1-84694-505-2 ebook: 978-1-78099-018-7

Punk Science
Inside the Mind of God
Manjir Samanta-Laughton
Many have experienced unexplainable phenomena; God, psychic abilities, extraordinary healing and angelic encounters. Can cutting-edge science actually explain phenomena previously thought of as 'paranormal'?
Paperback: 978-1-90504-793-2

The Vagabond Spirit of Poetry
Edward Clarke
Spend time with the wisest poets of the modern age and of the past, and let Edward Clarke remind you of the importance of poetry in our industrialized world.
Paperback: 978-1-78279-370-0 ebook: 978-1-78279-369-4

Readers of ebooks can buy or view any of these bestsellers by clicking on the live link in the title. Most titles are published in paperback and as an ebook. Paperbacks are available in traditional bookshops. Both print and ebook formats are available online.
Find more titles and sign up to our readers' newsletter at
http://www.johnhuntpublishing.com/non-fiction
Follow us on Facebook at
https://www.facebook.com/JHPNonFiction
and Twitter at https://twitter.com/JHPNonFiction